Head Down, Chin Up

The Secret Raver

ISBN: 978-1-916732-35-3

Published by:

i2i
PUBLISHING

www.i2ipublishing.co.uk
i2i Publishing, Manchester.

iii

Contents

iv

Intro

Here We Go Again, Hold Tight.

So, this is the second time I'm writing all this because of what happened when I got bail from Guildford Crown Court. I was in Wandsworth Prison on a charge that had nothing to do with me. I had been extradited from Italy (Rome) to London (Heathrow) on an International Arrest Warrant from Interpol. Drug Trafficking on an international level. Importing a Class A drug. Anyway, more about that later.

While I was in prison on remand, one month in Rome and five months in London, I wrote 27 short stories and escapades about my life. When you get bail when you're in Court, you don't go back to jail, because you're half free. I had finished my story and had it all written down in a book in my cell. Instead of looking after your shit, those fucking wanker screws at Wandsworth grab a few things and then let scumbag cons, who are called magpies, and whose job is to clean out the cell, just rob whatever's there and throw out the rest. I had photos and all my letters that I never saw again, sentimental stuff and the book I had written. To both of you, screws and magpies, Fuck you, I've done it again!

1

When My Dad Left, '85

I was 14 at the time and I can remember it like yesterday. It came as a shock and it has affected me without a doubt, because these things shape you. I'm not sitting here crying about it as I write. I got over it years ago. My dad died fifteen years ago, and we had always got on. I still miss him. I was lying in the bath listening to music, a habit I got from him and something I still do. I could hear shouting and crying and then silence. He came in and told me to get out of the bath, because he needed to tell me something. I can't remember who was there but when he told us he was leaving because he was in love with someone else, it was shocking.

My mum ran out of the house and tried to kill herself. Well, she jumped in her Fiat 600 and drove into a tree at the end of the road, if that counts as a suicide mission! It was night time and we were running down the street thinking she could be seriously hurt. She was fine, she didn't even go to hospital, but the car was fucked, which was probably a good thing, it was yellow and a Fiat 600! So he left that evening and we'd see him at weekends; my mum was the one who suffered the most.

Even after what he'd done, we still couldn't wait to see him. He said, "When you're older, you'll understand." And I do. Not long after, my mum met someone else, an ex-military man called Dave. We called him the Colonel, not to his face though. I thought he was a prick, with a dodgy Freddie

Mercury moustache. We clashed, me more than my sister and my brother, thank God I was playing a lot of football and I was good too. I had started training and playing for Wimbledon, The Crazy Gang, what a good time.

2

The Crazy Gang, '87

Me and Graham went training at Plough Lane twice a week. We lived near each other in Hanworth. We had to get three buses, but we loved it. Young kids with not a care in the world and dreams to be the best footballer in our streets. I trained there all summer that year too as part of my work experience at college. As the nickname says, they were really CRAZY – some of the things I saw there were unbelievable, I can still hear "Fuck Off Harry" by the senior players when Dave 'Harry' Bassett told them they were going on a run around the park. Now this was a different time and a different game.

We used to train at Richardson Evans Park which is off the A3. It was a favourite stop off for lorry drivers looking for a nice fried breakfast. It's a big playing field, it's still used now, not by Wimbledon though. It's mad to think they were training there when they were playing in the old First Division against United, Liverpool, Arsenal, etc. Anybody could walk in and have a look about, as it's a public park! When Harry Bassett or Alan Gillette told them they were going on a run to start training, they'd be "Fucking Hell", "Fuck off Alan" but then they'd be off. A bunch of them, usually led by Dennis Wise, would hide in the bushes and wait for the last lap and then join the group again – none of us were going to say anything against the first team, you couldn't do that now! They used to come in on a Monday morning, have a fried breakfast and go training, stinking of alcohol.

They used to train in black bin liners to sweat it out. This was when you were out the door by lunchtime and free to do what you wanted for the rest of the day. Most of them went straight down the pub or the bookies or the snooker hall, or all three! There were some top players in that team, Dennis Wise, Vinnie Jones, John Fashanu, Glynn Hodges, who had a beautiful left foot, one of the best I've ever seen. And of course, Dave "Lurch" Beasant. As you can tell by his nickname, he was very tall and a very good goalie. An England international. I lobbed him once in training, I was only 16. Harry Bassett and Alan Gillette used to take the sessions, they would put the two goals on the edge of the 18-yard box, everyone had a number and when your number was called, you ran into the centre circle and depending where the ball landed you had to score against one of the keepers. In one goal was Lurch and in the other was the Reserves keeper Neil Sullivan, who went on to become the Spurs and Scotland keeper. Two very good keepers. Anyway, my number was called, and I ran into the centre circle, controlled the ball, saw Lurch off his line, turned and lobbed him. 'Arry picked up the ball and said, "I've seen it all now, everyone under the showers", the session was over. Legend. He had the piss taken out of him for ages for that, lobbed by a schoolboy!

We could watch the home games for free at Plough Lane, one of the perks. Once before a Liverpool game, Vinnie Jones and the gang had their stereo blasting out very loud. The Liverpool players were moaning, and someone complained.

Remember, this was a top team: Rush, Barnes, etc. The changing rooms were portakabins, I shit you not. I was in the corridor outside the changing room, Vinnie punched the wall, made some space and stuck his head through the hole and screamed to the Liverpool players, "Anyone who comes near me today, I'll break their fucking legs."

I'm sure it ended 1-1, I can't remember who scored but if it was Fash, he'd have been happy, he was on a grand a goal. In 1987!

3

Outside Heaven, '89

After Wimbledon let me go, I went to play for Hampton FC, which is now Hampton and Richmond Borough, who play in the Vanarama League South. I was there a couple of years but had started going out a lot and getting into Acid House. In 1987/88 a bunch of English DJs who had come back from Ibiza started club nights in London: Shoom, Spectrum, etc. I had gotten into the E scene quite quickly as I had a friend who gave me as many as I wanted. I was paying £12 for them then and sold them on for £20/25. As we got into 1989 more clubs and more raves were starting, so business was good. It was 1988 that I took coke for the first time, it was in the Hammersmith Palais at a Gatecrashers Ball. They were organised by a posh bloke whose family owned the house in the TV series To the Manor Born, where he held a few balls and raves too. His name was Jeremy. At the balls everyone dressed up all smart and just went fucking mental. Good times.

So, it was on a toilet seat in a crowded cubicle that I started my relationship with the old Devil's Dandruff. Me and my mate Roy were partners in the E game and with the money we were making, we bought coke. Roy's dad was in a rock band in the 70s and 80s and knew a lot of people in the music business and could get good gear. It was £60 a gramme but would last forever. I remember massive wraps with a yellowish colour, it was lovely. And moreish. One night we were outside Heaven nightclub in London. We had gone there to serve up but just before we went in, we wanted a sniff. I stashed the pills I had, about 200, in a building site across from Heaven. I'd come and get them when I needed them, 50 at a time. So me and Roy jumped over a little gate of a town house and walked down the stairs to the basement flat for a little livener before going in. So it was wrap out, a little chop and then a big corner off a card. Bang.

As we jumped back over the gate, two look-alike ravers with moody tracksuits and rucksacks, jumped on us, with their police I.D. cards out. They shone their torches in our faces and started asking questions, a police car pulled up with back up. Bollox, I thought. I had about 15 pills in my pocket and as they were talking to us, I threw them on the floor. They saw the pills and picked them up, while I was pleading innocence. I can't remember if Roy threw the coke or not, but we were going to Bow Street police station. Handcuffs on in the back of the car, I could feel I still had some pills in my back pocket. I couldn't throw them in the car as I was saying I knew nothing of the pills they found in the gutter. I gave two to Roy and I necked two. The E's were called Cali's or Biscuits, they were big white pills with a line down the middle, so you could break it in half. Half first and then another half later, "Get right on one matey" was a song back in the day that explained this. That was when E's were E's and the quality was high. Later on, the quality went down and you would have to take more to get a buzz. Anyway, these were fucking strong. 20 minutes later I was fucked, my jaw was all over the gaff and I was rushing my nuts off on my own in a cell. I couldn't stand still, up and down the cell, rocking. Roy was next door, so we were talking together.

E-ing each other up, boosting our buzz. Then the interview. Roy had been released without charge because they had nothing on him, the slippery cunt. I was trying to hold it down as much as I could but being off your nut on two biscuits and sitting at a desk with two Old Bill in front of you is not easy, especially when one of them tells you he knows your dad! Well, that fucking ruined my buzz! My old man was in the Met Police for 28 years, ending his career as a Detective Constable. I was 18 then and fuck knows why they insisted on phoning my dad and my mum (who had split up years ago) at 2am, to tell them what had happened. Wankers.

I was charged with possession of Ecstasy, about 10 pills and told to attend Bow Street Mags Court in a few days. They let me out at about 5am – I had come down by then. When I walked out, I saw two mates of mine, Scotty and Samson had come to get me after Heaven. Scotty was from Somerstown near Kings Cross, we used to drink together down The Cock Tavern there, top pub. We were all big Arsenal fans and go to football together. Five pints of Snakebite and blackcurrant and then down to Highbury, good fucking times man. I saw some crazy shit in the Cock Tavern, bananas. Madness! After getting out of the station I went back to Heaven to get the Garys I had stashed, good job I had done too! We got there before the builders came, necked a couple each and went back to Scotty's flat to talk poo and wait for the Cock Tavern to open. As you do. When I went back to court, the old judge didn't have a fucking clue what Ecstasy were, but fined me anyway, the old bastard! £300. "I'll pay that now Your Honour, got a plane to catch."

4

Fun City – Arsenal, '89

Probably one of the best Friday nights ever. The famous 1989 title decider between Liverpool and Arsenal was played on a Friday evening at 8pm. This game would decide the old First Division title. Arsenal had to win by 2 clear goals in the last game of the season. At Liverpool. Nobody thought we could do it, not even my brother, who left Anfield five minutes before the end. The Knob! Haha. I was at my girlfriend's flat in Kew; her mum had a lovely flat above a shop near Kew Gardens train station. My girlfriend's twin sister was going out with a mate of mine, John, so we were all watching it together. My mate John was West Ham. I can't remember who he wanted to win, but I didn't care as Alan 'Smudger' Smith put us ahead, but we needed another to win on goal difference. I can still see that prick Steve McMahon shaking his fist, telling his teammates there was only a minute to go. They were already celebrating, fucking brilliant.

Lukic threw the ball to Dixon, who smashed it up to Smith who headed it on to Thomas who with a bit of luck went running through and scored. Like every other Arsenal fan, I went fucking mental, jumping up and down like a lunatic. We had waited since 1971 for this. Tonight at Shaftesbury's would be a good night. Friday night was Fun City at Shaftesbury's on Shaftesbury Avenue. A bloke called Jeremy, who used to do the balls ran it, and it was a top night out. I was a Gold Card member because we used to help him with 'Energy' at the raves. All my friends would be there and also my Arsenal mates. We ran fucking riot in there that night, fucking funny. Jumping up and down on the tables singing Arsenal songs, in and out of the toilets. I remember a bouncer came up to me and asked me to calm everyone down a bit please! I was 18. We did have a good little firm there though. Samson, Scotty, Walker, John, Little Andy, Brighton Barry, all Arsenal and well known round the West End. Paul 'Trouble' Anderson was rocking the dance floor. We had some top nights there, a couple of bad nights too.

Once when we were leaving the club me and my partner Roy were attacked with baseball bats. They chased Roy down the street, but he was quite fast when he wanted to be. One of them came up to me and told me they were after him and not me, I found out after why. We were getting our pills laid on and I found out that instead of paying the dealer, he was keeping the money and sticking it up his nose. We had a big fall out after that. That same night at Fun City when Arsenal won the title some bloke gave me a nut nut Acid tab. Me and John done half each, fucking freaked the shit out of me. One of the longest days of my life that was, luckily John was on the same trip, so we helped each other out – it was like being in a cartoon. Next time I see that dealer at Fun City, I'll kill him.

5

Effingham, Energy Rave, '89

What a motley crew. We were having it large that night, we left in Jon's Sierra from Richmond on our way to one of the big raves of the year. Energy in Effingham, Surrey, just off the M25. Jon was driving me, Scoots, Roy and Yinks. We had all been working for Jeremy, he was the promoter and we had been selling tickets for him for the last few months. I was with a girl at the time and her dad owned a big printing firm. Bingo! I gave him a book of tickets I had got from Jeremy and asked him to do another two hundred tickets, exactly the same: two books of a hundred tickets. You couldn't tell the difference, back then there wasn't the kind of controls there are now. We were selling them all over London, outside clothes shop and record shops that were selling the official tickets, ours were obviously cheaper.

Back to the car, we left Richmond after a few drinks and a few lines. Someone was being greedy, there's always one, who sniffs more and drinks more than the others. Roy was sitting in the back of the car; he was my partner in the pill game. Drinking cans of beer like water until he started gagging, too much sniff and beer, he got the window open in time and he was throwing up down the side of the car. Jon was not happy and nor were we as little bits were flying back in the car, we were crying with laughter, Roy with beer in hand, dribbling with sick and tears running down his eyes from gagging so much. Funny.

As we got closer to the field where the rave was, we could see the security and the long line of cars waiting to get into the car park. The music was already pumping. Just warming up. We had guest list passes, so security didn't give us any grief, didn't even check us as we slipped in with two hundred pills. Before we went into the rave, we had gone around the cars selling the rest of the moody tickets. There wasn't one left, job done. So now we were just thinking of selling the Cali's we had. Adamski was the headliner, he had a couple of big hits back in the day but there were loads of top DJs: Oakenfold, Fabio, Nicki Holloway, etc. – a lot of the Fun City crew. It was banging, loads of people looking for E's. We had to keep going back to the car to drop money off, what with ticket money and E money, we had 2 plastic bags full of cash stuffed in the boot of Jon's car. Good job nobody saw us! We finished the pills and ate some too, we didn't even stay till the end. Back to Richmond to count the money. Energy '89. E safe.

6

A Bottle in the Face, '90

Having a bottle smashed in your face is not nice. Especially on Xmas Eve and by someone you know. I was from Twickenham, and I knew a lot of people. The bloke who bottled me was one of the younger crew who hung around Twickenham. We were a bit older and the girls from the younger crew were always trying to hang around with us, so it was for this reason I was talking to a girl in a pub on Xmas Eve in Twickers. I can't even remember how it started but he was jealous for some reason and started being mouthy. After being told to fuck off, and a bit of pushing, he stuck a bottle in my face and legged it. The little cunt.

After things calmed down, me, my brother and my cousin went looking for him. They used to hang around in a park not far from where we were, so that's where we went. There were a few of them there but no sign of him. I let them know that this wasn't finished and carried myself off to the hospital. We got home in the early hours of Xmas morning, not a nice sight for my nan and parents, but there you go, it is what it is, until it isn't.

I wanted revenge, so Xmas day was spent plotting what to do and getting in contact with a few friends. Mostly 'The Barmy Army' from Teddington, a group of friends who wanted to help. One of them had a Transit van so we arranged to meet in a pub in Tedds, have a few drinks, a couple of bumps and head over to Twickers. Baseball bats were the choice of weapon. I had borrowed an aluminium one off my brother-in-law, I thought it'd be easier to wash the blood off afterwards.

We were all buzzing as we got in the van outside The Red Lion. There were about ten of us in the back and three in the front. Screams of 'We're the Barmy Teddington Army' were coming out of the van as we made our way to the pub in Twickers. A few beers and a few lines always makes you happy and up for a row! I had told everyone the M.O.: we'd pull up outside the pub, I'd go in and call out the bloke who glassed me, as he walks out I'd hit him round the head with a baseball bat. Someone obviously didn't understand! Darren had got out for a piss at the beginning of the road, we drove up about 50 metres to the pub and stopped the van. I've gone in, seen the bloke and told him to come outside for a straightener.

As I've walked out, Darren's come pushing past me into the pub and started hitting anything in his way. All hell broke loose. People running left, right and centre trying to escape. The people behind the bar ran upstairs screaming, the boy I was after escaped out the back door not to be seen in Twickenham for a long time. All the rest of my lot were running around the pub hitting anyone they found. A couple of people inside were good friends of mine so they were spared. People were lying all over the pub.

As quick as it had started, it was over. We jumped back in the van and went back to Teddington for a drink to celebrate. Everyone was buzzing, adrenalin was high. When we got back to the Lion, everyone was going on about what they did and how it went down. Beer, toilet, beer, toilet, same old routine. Anyway, it was my birthday so we had a double reason to celebrate. "We're the Barmy Teddington Army" La La La La

7

Mad Mick from Moss Side, '90

The heat hits you like a hairdryer in your face. Me, Paul and Max had saved up to buy a ticket from Gatwick one-way to L.A.-Hawaii-Auckland and dropped off in Sydney. I spunked all my money in six weeks and flew back to London, but that's another story. So, we arrived in L.A. with our backpacks full and our heads full of dreams. I had the address of my sister's best friend, who lived in L.A. Outside LAX there were lots of people handing out flyers for illegal hostels. We grabbed one from a girl just to be polite, but we were off to Gemma's. We got talking to a couple of people who lived in L.A., and they said we could jump in their truck, and they'd drop us off. American hospitality.

Brilliant. Someone forgot to tell us that Gemma had moved, it was getting dark, and we had nowhere to stay. So we went to the pub! Standard. After crying in our Bud's for a bit we started looking on the bright side of things. We were in L.A. Beer, women, drugs, we just needed somewhere to sleep. Paul pulled out the flyer the girl gave us at LAX. A hostel in Venice Beach. Sounds good. We got chatting to a few people in the bar and they offered to take us there. Another touch. It was a big apartment above a Chinese dry cleaners.

Mad Mick from Moss Side was the boss of the hostel, it was his thing, he had rented the place and turned it into a hostel for like-minded travellers. We all became friends very quickly. He was five foot nothing, didn't stop talking, had a big heart and wasn't scared of anything or anyone. He was from Manchester, as he liked to remind us often, as Madchester was in full flow. The Happy Mondays were touring L.A. while we were there with Paul Oakenfold, the DJ who produced their hit album 'Pills, Thrills and Bellyaches'. Oakey used to get bang on it with us back in the day at Heaven. We used to have a top laugh with Mad Mick, we used to do odd jobs for him around the house to pay less rent. We didn't have a lot of money, so we used to hit the pubs at Happy Hour to eat for free. We used to go to the Green Onion in Marina del Rey and smash their buffet. We'd buy one drink and nut straight into the food. It was banging, all types of food: tacos, pasta, hot dogs, the lot.

During Italia 90 we used to go to a pub called 2 Drops of Scotch. On match days it was packed; when we beat Cameroon the whole pub did the conga across the main street outside the pub. The Yanks had never seen anything like it. There was a massive ex-pat scene in Santa Monica, and everyone would get down the pub for the games. It went off a few times, the English against the Scots, the banter would get out of hand and a few glasses would fly, all good fun. We used to go with Mick into Compton where he went boxing, a very dangerous place but he was respected there so we were fine with him. We'd stop at the traffic lights at night on the way back, the streets would seem empty but as soon as the van stopped, loads of little gang-bangers would jump out from behind cars and lamp posts to try and jack the van, crazy.

Me, Paul, Max and Fred, another mate from London who had come to visit us for a bit, went to see Nelson Mandela. He had been released from prison after 27 years and was doing his world tour to raise money for the cause. It was at the Coliseum Baseball Park in downtown L.A. There were about 70,000 people there and I swear we were the only white people there. Looking around all you could see were coloured people. "I damn the white man"..."The white man can't dance" shouted Jesse Jackson. Shit, I thought, we were in the wrong place, but there was never a hint of trouble. Ice T and other rappers and Afro-American singers and actors took to the stage to show their support for Mandela. When the great man came on stage, he got a 20-minute standing ovation. One man's freedom fighter is another man's terrorist. What a night. Just to top it off, Mad Mick was supposed to be meeting us at a pre-arranged place and time. He wasn't there, walking around L.A after midnight is not a good look, especially being white. We found him a bar arguing with someone over a game of pool. Mad Mick from Moss Side. Legend!

8

Ham, '91

Non-stop fighting when we were kids, I don't know how we found time to do anything else. We were from Twickenham and wherever you went, Kingston, Hounslow, there was always trouble with the locals. You'd go to parties and there'd always be problems. We would move around in a big group, boys and girls, about 20 of us. When there's that many of you, it's bound to cause a commotion. My mum had bought a hairdressers in Ham, so I was always over there. This upset the locals, a weird, inbred bunch. I was the New Kid on the Block and they couldn't handle it. Every time I went over there it was fisticuffs. Once I was on the 71 bus from Kingston to Ham, a packed bus, it was rush hour and me and my brother were minding our own business upstairs, when I got a kick to the side of the head. Little fucker, it was Billy, again. Every time we saw each other we had a row, wherever we were. I jumped up to see him and all his boys down the back of the bus. I grabbed him and started smashing his head off the railings, the metal bits on top of the chairs. We got kicked off the bus but continued to fight when I saw him outside my mum's shop. My mum came out and split that up. She knew all of the boys because they were always hanging around the cafe next door to her shop.

I'd had straighteners with every one of their top boys by now; we didn't like each other. One night we went drinking in a pub in Richmond, near the station.

A few of the older Ham boys were in there and we were chatting, having a bit of banter, when it got out of hand. One of their so-called top boys went for me and I punched him straight in the face, it all went off. After the bouncers got involved and it all moved outside, he started walking off towards the train station. I followed him and I saw him on the pay phone, he had his little black book out and said he'd phoned his boys and they were coming. He walked towards me, now I've grown up with a motto given to me by my uncle, 'Hit first, ask questions later'. So I punched him, as he's going down I kicked him in the head. 30 years have passed and I'm not proud of it, but it happened. He fell on the floor in the middle of the foyer in the station. He ended up in a coma for a few days, but he came out ok.

While he was in hospital his boys came looking for me. They turned up at my sister's house where I was living at the time. They didn't find me because I had gone out, my best mate was looking after my nephew, he was seeing my cousin at the time. They pulled up in a couple of cars and started kicking the door and smashing the windows, they were calling my name, but I wasn't in. My nephew was only young, about three, and obviously was very scared as was my cousin. My mate knew most of them because his mum lived in Ham, and he tried to talk to them. As he opened the door one of them tried to get in, my mate just smashed him in the face and he was gone, straight out the door. They tried to storm the house, but my mate had his back against the stairs and his feet against the door, so they couldn't get in. The police arrived and they legged it.

I wasn't happy, bringing it to my sister's house was not on, so something had to be done. A couple of days later I borrowed a car from a work friend and with my brother, two cousins and some friends drove over to Ham to sort out a few things. I don't know if they found about it, but we walked straight into an ambush. Our car was attacked on one of the streets inside Ham. They came from everywhere, over walls, from behind trees, we were well outnumbered, so everyone just ran. A good captain knows when to fight, and when not to. I stopped in the middle of the road, one of their boys who I knew well came over to tell me to leg it. I was with Darren, my best mate's brother, we sort of got boxed in against a wall. They arrived. Have you ever been hit over the head with a baseball bat? It hurts. But it fucking livens you up as well. They had knives and baseball bats. And they were using them, they had stabbed Darren on the arse, and he was going down. I grabbed him so he didn't go to the floor, because if that happens, you're fucked. The good thing about lots of people attacking you is that there are no clear shots.

Everyone gets in the way of everybody. Although some little cunt stabbed me twice in the side, it had gone through my Schott leather jacket and the lining too. I grabbed hold of one of them and stuck my finger right in his eye, I could have popped it if I wanted. Anyway, until the police came, we got battered. God knows who called the Old Bill, but thanks! I got stabbed in the back twice and smashed all over with a baseball bat. I would see the people who stabbed me in the future, I didn't let that go. Darren got stabbed in the arse and beaten too. It was off to Kingston Hospital for us.

Nothing serious and we were sent home. My workmate's car was fucked and the others were nowhere to be seen.

9

Porky's, '91. Sydney

If you go to Sydney, you have to go to King's Cross, the city's red-light district. And you must visit Porky's, although I think it's closed down now. In 1991 I flew out to Sydney to meet up with my friends Paul and Max, who had continued their travels from L.A. to Hawaii and then N.Z. Now they were on the last stop of their trip, Sydney. They had a little two bed flat in Darlinghurst, not a very nice area but it was somewhere to get our heads down as we were never in anyway. I had some brilliant times in Sydney and met some top people. Never brought anyone back to the flat though, because it was a dump. When you turned the lights on the whole house moved because of the cockroaches, little fuckers. The walls literally moved when the lights went on, and when you slept, you'd feel them in your ears and nose, disgusting.

My mate Fred had his Nike Air Jordans stolen from the windowsill, his trainers stunk so we insisted he left them on the windowsill. Some little fucker climbed the drainpipe and had them away. Another time we were all watching TV when someone kicked our door down, ran in and grabbed the TV. He didn't see us, we all just looked at each other in shock, he grabbed the TV and legged it, he didn't make it out of the block. We gave him a few slaps and let him go. Fucking funny. My mate Max worked the day shift in Porky's, he worked the bar, put the dirty films on and generally done whatever was needed, Porky's was a brothel. It's legal in Australia, or at least it was then. At night it was packed, especially at weekends, full of stag do's, hen nights. There was a live sex show, lesbian show, snake show, it was brilliant.

So when Max told me they were looking for a bar man, I was straight in there. At night it was a different story, all the best girls worked at night, all the rough ones during the day with Max. It was like the graveyard shift but the other way around. It was a seedy place but one of the higher end brothels in Kings X. It was owned by two Sicilian brothers, they had three nite-spots in the X. Kings X is one long street called Darlinghurst Rd. Down this one street are bars, fast food places, restaurants and strip clubs/brothels, discos, pubs. It had everything. Anyone visiting Sydney went to Kings X. I got on really well with Nick, who ran the bar, he was a Hells Angel. They all used to come in with their gear on, and it was drinks all round. On the house. He was good like that, he always told me that if my mates came in to give them some drinks, no problem. My mates were always propping up the bar. It was only a small bar, no pints, just cans of beer and spirits. The bar was about 6ft wide, so most of the time it was just me. Fucking had some top times in there.

Bumped into lots of people from back home too. I'd be working when I'd hear "Fucking hell, what are you doing here?"

"Well, I'm working, what the fuck are you doing here?" Michael Hutchence from INXS used to get in there at least once a week. Good times. The girls walked around in their lingerie and high heels. This was how it worked. The girls worked the floor, chatting to blokes and getting them to buy them drinks. The more drinks their punters bought, there was more money for them at the end of the night. I had to keep a list of all the drinks the girls had. The friendlier ones had the longer list, obviously. The girls were always trying to get me upstairs for a freebie. You scratch my back and I'll scratch yours love. It wasn't long before I started seeing one of the girls. I was with her non-stop for about three or four months. It's bad but I can't remember her name. She had two names as well. One was her work name and one her real name, I can't remember either.

So they'd get the punters pissed, making them spend money at the bar and then take them upstairs to one of the rooms. Hygiene wasn't very big at Porky's, so you could have a shower or a bath, jacuzzi, that type of thing. I found some fat fucker dead in one of the toilets, they probably fucked him to death. Or probably not, as one of their things was Trick Sex. They'd take a punter upstairs, two girls, get him on the floor or on the bed, one would get on top of him and pretend to ride him while using her hand behind her back to wank him off. Most were so pissed they didn't realise.

While this was happening, the other girl was going through his wallet, stealing money, and putting the credit cards through the old fashioned machines. Nobody's going to the police when they realise they'd been robbed. They don't want the wife finding out. We'd finish work about 4am and then go drinking in Kings X. It was brilliant because wherever you went, they'd know I was the barman at Porky's and give me free drinks or we'd get in the clubs on the guest list.

I'd repay the favour when they came to Porky's. The girl I was with would earn on average a grand a night, at weekends more. She'd spoil me, coke every night, pills, restaurants, hotels, it was brilliant because I only worked two nights a week, so I didn't have a lot of money. When she was sleeping, I'd nick $50 out of her bag, I know it's out of order, but I was polo, her bag would be full of notes. All the girls who worked nights were very pale faced. They'd sleep all day and go back out in the evening to work, so they didn't see any sunlight. We'd go back to hers in the morning, fuck about for a bit and then sleep, get up about 4pm, go to a restaurant and then crack on again. Brilliant. She was lovely, when I left to go travelling with Max, she gave me $1,000 in cash. I just can't remember her name!

10

Koh Phangan, '91

When we left Sydney, me and Max headed up the East Coast of Oz making our way to Darwin to fly to Bali. I had to have a hospital trip in Cairns for the face injuries I got in Sydney. The night before we left, all our friends got together for a last night out and a send-off. Fuck knows what happened, but we were in a bar with a team of Maori rugby players. All I remember is me throwing a beer bottle into their crowd. Big mistake. They used my head like one of their rugby balls. I've got a picture somewhere of my head the morning after. Down one side it's blown up like a balloon. Not a very good sending off. My fault anyway, a bit of advice, don't start on a group of Maori rugby players!

Anyway, we were on our way to Thailand to meet up with some friends of ours, who we had met in Sydney. A good crowd, mostly Arsenal fans from Loughton in Essex. Me and Max flew to Bali, travelled up Indonesia, stayed a couple of nights in Singapore and then by bus and train we headed through Malaysia to South Thailand. South Thailand is beautiful, we stayed on a few islands in Krabi. One of the islands has now been taken over by an American hotel company, Phra Ngan Beach in Krabi. You have to walk or swim through the rocks to get to Railay Beach. One of the most beautiful beaches in the world. We were making our way to Bangkok to meet the boys. The meeting place for travellers was the Khao San Road, one long street full of bars, restaurants, b&bs, pubs, massage parlours, travel agents, etc. After a couple of heavy nights in Bangkok we set off for Koh Samui. We all travelled together in small mini vans that leave Bangkok every day for the beautiful island of Koh Samui, from Samui we were going to get a boat to Koh Phangan for the famous Full Moon party. The boat journey was about 30 minutes and was brilliant. That first time in Thailand everything was so cheap, in Samui a bungalow with a double bed and a little balcony on the beach cost 40 baht, which was a £1. Thai green curry cost about 30p and a bottle of whiskey with Coca-Cola and ice about £1.50. With a tenner a day you lived like a king. They soon realised though; the next two times I went they had put the prices well up.

When we got to Koh Phangan we got settled in our bungalows and went out for dinner. Tonight was the famous Full Moon party, a party on the beach started by a few hippies until it took on a life of its own. It's now world famous. We thought we'd get in the mood with a mushroom omelette. A Magic Mushroom Omelette. We found this restaurant made of wood on stilts, like a lot of the bars and restaurants there. We all ordered an omelette and a few beers, I don't know why but they left me to sort out the bill. I'd like to think it's my ability in maths! Everyone threw in their money, and it was left to me to count it and pay the lovely Thai women who had served us. I was fucked. And this is where things took a turn for the worse. They kicked in, The Shooms. I was all over the place, I couldn't even pick up the money off the table, giggling on my hands and knees trying to grab the money that was falling through the 4 by 2s on to the sand below. I was on my own. So off I went under the restaurant crawling on all fours, looking for the cash. God knows how I paid, because I was in another world, but I did and I fucked off, quickly. I walked out of the restaurant and instead of turning right towards the beach and the party, I turned left into the forest towards a bar that was covered in fluorescent lights. It looked inviting. Anyone who has done shooms will understand. I stood captivated by it for a bit, drank a beer, fuck knows how I asked for it, and then decided I needed a piss. I took off into the forest, fascinated by the sounds and the lights and the fucking flying monkeys over my head. My brain was full of magic mushrooms. I found a suitable tree and stood there for 2 hours with 'pesce in mano' until my friends found me. I was hugging the tree for over 2 hours out of my nut. They took me back to the party and we stayed up all night drinking Thai whiskey, which they say is loaded with amphetamines. Tops.

11

HMP The Mount. How and Why, '92

We got back from Thailand in October and nearing Xmas I went to a party in a pub, this was late '91. We were all in there and we were having a laugh when I saw my brother having an argument at the bar. Not minding my own business, I went over to see what was happening. It all happened very quickly, and the bloke got a pint glass in his face. This is one incident that could have and should have been avoided. But shit happens. I got arrested at the local hospital, where we both ended up – me for a cut on my hand that needed an operation (I nearly lost the use of my right hand), and the bloke for a big cut on his face and neck. Not very nice.

I was released on bail and told to attend court. I was going not guilty but the cut on my hand was a bit of a giveaway. I was charged with GBH Sec 18, which could get you life in jail. Once the court case started and we saw the evidence against me, I changed my plea to guilty, this way the judge would hopefully thank me for not wasting public money and time at court. And give me less time in the Big House. Good family, very sorry, first offence, I got two years. I'd do a year exactly. The night before I got sentenced, I was at a mate's house in Tedds, me and some mates stayed up all night discussing how long I'd get, the cunts were taking bets. Isleworth Crown Court in the morning and off to the Scrubs. When you're young you don't give a fuck but seeing that old Victorian building was a wake-up call.

The journey from court to prison was a killer, a feeling I'll never forget. Stuck in a sweat box for the first time, you can see out but they can't see us. It was a Friday afternoon and looking out of the window, seeing all the people who had just finished work and heading home or to the pub, was a nightmare. What the fuck had I done. I'd have given anything to swap places with one of them. That's when it really hit me, I felt like shit, and staying up all night on the chop chop didn't fucking help! The first night's the worst. You wake up in the morning and you don't know where you are. I was banged up with a Muslim and he was praying to his God when I woke up. When the doors opened, he went out and I helped myself to some of his toothpaste, sorry mate, shouldn't have but there you go, needs must.

After the induction they gave me a job in the kitchen, with the LIFERS! I think the screws were trying to teach me a lesson. I didn't have any problems, I got to know a few of them but everyone kept themselves to themselves. "Head down, chin up" my old mate Jim told me. That was my motto and a bit of sound advice. It was the beginning of November now and working in the kitchen was a godsend. First thing, it was hot, Victorian prisons in the winter are cold. Most of the old prisons are cold in winter but the Scrubs was freezing. So being in the kitchen was lovely, plus you could eat what you wanted as you were cooking. You used to get an English breakfast back then, not now, all muesli bars and cornflakes. Bollox. Hot toast and chipolatas. Banging.

After a few weeks there I was given my cat C

and told I was off to The Mount prison in Hemel Hempstead. There was a minibus full of us from the Scrubs, we were in good spirits, a cat C prison meant more freedom and home leaves! The Mount was like a Boys Club, I had some top times in there and met some good people. Everyone had to go to work or do some type of education, I opted for a cleaning course with my next door neighbour and new mate, Italian Paul from Hoxton, a small but strong Italian kid who was inside for putting a hammer over someone's head at a petrol station. The teacher brought us in drinks and let us use the phone, plus I got a City and Guilds Diploma!

I was the new star of the football team too, we used to train twice a week and then a team would come in on Saturdays, no away games in our league for us! It was nice to get out on to the pitch and forget about everything. A couple of players had tried to get over the fence while playing, not for me, too much hard work, fucking thing is well high. Saturdays were the best days because we would play a game, have a shower and then off to a visit. We'd get alcohol dropped off outside in the gardens and one of the inmates who worked outside would bring it in. My mates would come up on a visit and it was so easy to smuggle in sniff and puff, passed over on the visit or in a parcel with the alcohol. I'd sell the puff for phonecards and have a little party in my cell on Saturday night. Good times. We had a television in our cells, kettles, stereos, a toilet and a sink! We had our own duvets and curtains from home sent in, rugs on the floor, a proper little studio flat. I'd get lots of people coming in to say hello and have a cup of tea or whiskey on a sat evening.

One of the black boys I had met on the bus coming from the Scrubs would come and see me, I don't think he had much, and he loved all my home comforts. Anyway, I lent him one of my Walkmans, I had three so no drama. I was queuing up for dinner one day when someone told me that matey had sold my Walkman or pawned it for a bit of puff. I found him and told him to come to my cell after dinner for a cup of tea. As soon as he walked in my cell I headbutted him straight on the nose; he went down, and I gave him a few kicks. He got up and ran out of my cell, now my cell was the last on the wing, right at the end on the left. Paul next door had heard it all going off and was coming to see if all was good, the black kid ran past him, Paul tripped him up and gave him a boot. All the way out of the wing he got kicked and slapped; the next day he went down the block and got himself shipped out.

We had some really good times there, there were more drugs in there than outside, it was in the Mount that I saw heroin for the first time. A lot of people were smoking it, "Chasing the Dragon" as it's called. It was cheap and it made you feel good, and it makes your bird go quicker, so they say! You couldn't sniff inside, I mean you could and I did, loads. But being stuck in your cell with 3 grammes of coke is not good. It was ok when the doors are open, and you share it about with friends and have a drink but when the doors shut and it's 3am is not nice. The amount of gear I threw down the toilet! The other good thing about the Mount was you could get a day release a month after being there. People would ask for a day out to go and buy trainers, it was crazy. One of the Knightsbridge safe deposit robbers had fucked things for everyone for a bit; he got out for a day and was pictured by the Sun sitting outside a posh bar with a page 3 girl and drinking champagne – who said crime doesn't pay? That stopped the day releases for a bit, and the chaps weren't happy! I think he got slapped for that when he came back, and he had to change prison.

I got out to see my nan who was dying, I think I stayed with her for an hour and then went down the pub with my mates. Not very nice but she was happy to see me and happy knowing I had a bit of freedom for a bit. I got my mum to phone the jail and ask for an extension until the next day as I was so upset, they said yes. Sweet. Straight up West that night. I cracked on the next day and my mates dropped me off at the prison for 5pm. I was fucked, I rolled out of the car and was helped back to my cell by two screws, I couldn't remember a thing. I woke up the next day and there was money all over the floor, money I had smuggled in. I had a shower, grabbed Paul and we went straight upstairs to the Yardies to get some bones. Dem bones, Dem bones! After a few months I got my Cat D and I was off. Spring Hill here I come.

12

Spring Hill, '93

So I was off to Spring Hill, a lovely open prison in the Buckinghamshire countryside. I was let out of The Mount on the Friday for a weekend release and told to present myself Monday afternoon in Aylesbury. When I got there, they gave me all the shit about this being an open prison and the responsibility is on you, blah blah blah. They showed me to a barrack-like dormitory, like you see in old Victorian films. Fucking depressing. Luckily enough I had a bed next to an interesting fella from Wembley. A fucking top man who became a very good friend. Cris from Wembley. In Spring Hill, at least back then, it was divided in to two parts, Beverly Hills and the Bronx. We had just arrived so we were in the Bronx. There was an official waiting list and an unofficial waiting list to get up to Beverly Hills, depending on who you knew. Beverly Hills were new portakabins with 12 double rooms, a communal TV area, showers, a kitchen and toilets. All the old boys and the faces were in Beverly Hills, obviously. We were scumming it in the Bronx.

Now I didn't know but Cris's dad was a bit of an OG, old school bank robber, he was a member of the firm known as the Wembley Mob, who used to take the tops off of security vans with chainsaws. Heavy armed robbers from the 70s and 80s. All the old faces would speak to Cris and ask about his dad, so Cris asked them about getting us up to the Hills. We waited about two days, and we were up there.

Touch. Pat Tate, who was killed in the Range Rover murders was in our cabin. He was like a gentle giant, very quiet, he used to help me in the gym, he seemed like a nice person. We had some funny times there. We used to skip out at night and go to the local pub. Every weekend we had a home release, Saturday or Sunday, you could choose. A few of us would get together and organise what we had to bring back. One of us would get the food, one the alcohol and so on. Near the prison was a little bridge and we'd drop off the alcohol underneath it on the way back before we'd re-enter, crates of beers, bottles of spirits, everything. At night after the last roll call, we'd dress up in black, me, Cris and Italian Paul who had followed me to Spring Hill when he got his Cat D. Dressed up in dark clothes and with balaclavas on, we'd go on a mission to bring back the alcohol and the other contraband.

Spring Hill is surrounded by countryside, we had to get through the fields to the bridge. It was pitch black and very cold most of the time. We didn't even have a torch and if it had been raining it was a nightmare. One night we left to get our loot and it was pissing down, fucking torrential rain, but nothing was stopping us. We waited 10 minutes after the screw went and made our way out the back door of the cabin, the back of the cabin backed on to a field, so it was over the fence and off we go. Running through the fields when you are knee high in mud is fucking difficult, but we were jumping over fences like hurdles, it was pissing down. We knew where we were going but couldn't see a fucking thing and it was quite foggy too.

Cris jumped over a fence, caught his foot as he was going over and falls flat on his face in mud and cow shit, that was everywhere. Me and Paul were pissing ourselves with laughter until we saw what looked like a cow. With all the noise we were making, we'd pissed it off. As it got nearer, we could see it had horns, fuck this. It started making noises and charged us, our laughter and Cris's fall had awoken the beast! You have never seen three people run so fast, but the problem was the mud, it stuck to you like glue, you could feel the fat bastard right behind us, you could smell it, but we were gone. We got to the fence and flew over it headfirst. We were covered in mud and cow shit, but I have never laughed so much and for so long, we were literally crying. Fucking freezing cold, stinking of shit but nothing was getting in the way of our goods. On the way back it was hard work with the heavy bags and we had to take a different route to avoid our friendly Bull. We'd knock three times on the back door of the cabin and a couple of cons would be ready at the door with a bucket and mop. As soon as we were in it was boots off, and one of the lags was behind us mopping the floor up, to not leave a trace. Straight in the showers then some nice food, well that was the plan, but we just went straight to pudding and got on the chop chop. Whenever somebody went out for the day, we'd take it in turns to get the sniff and the bones in. Good times.

We got shipped out of Spring Hill in the end, we beat up a Pakistani bloke who had raped his niece. We got balaclavaed up and ran down the Bronx one night into his dormitory and beat the fuck out of him. Me and Paul took the rap for that as Cris was being released in a couple of weeks, so he had to keep his nose clean. I had slapped Pat Tate's cell mate up too, so it was all coming a bit on top, he owed Cris some phonecards but refused to pay so I ran in his cell, Pat was on his bed and fucking jumped, but fair play he didn't get involved. So I done the last bit of my bird at Bullingdon, luckily no days were added on for bad behaviour. Bullingdon was a cat B Prison not far from Spring Hill. I had a few weeks left and got banged up with a Pakistani bloke, we got on fine, turned out to be a cool geezer. Him and his boys used to cook up for dinner, so the time went well. Just kept my nose clean and waited for the door to open for the last time. My old man picked me up, I hadn't seen a lot of him in the last year, with him being a DC in the Met!

13

My Scar '95. Twickers

If you met me, you'd see that I've got a scar from behind my ear across my face, a long straight line done by an ex-friend, also two scars on the same side of the face done by the bottle attack I've spoken about. Thank God for the NHS, eh? This story is difficult to write about for me because I made a mistake but what he done and how he done it, was out of order. It was about 11am and the bell went at my mum's house, I went downstairs and at the door was a friend I hadn't seen for a long time with me being in jail and he had been away too. I knew he had the hump with me and wanted to see me, we had mutual friends who had livened me up.

He asked me to go for a drive with him, I said I'd get my jacket and come. I went to a drawer in the kitchen and picked up a hammer, I thought we'd be having a fist fight, I knew he could have a row, so I put the hammer back. Fucking wish I'd have taken it with me now. We drove to a spot where he used to live in Twickers. I knew the area well, I grew up there. I said there was a park around the corner, we could go there for a straightener. As I get out of his little van to lead the way, he came from behind me and put his arm around my neck and cut my face. It didn't hurt but I could see the blood. I needed a tool, so I went looking for something, anything. I found some milk bottles, picked them up and threw them at him. He came at me again, I put up my hand and he cut my finger. He jumped in his van and drove off. I was losing a lot of blood, my mum had a hairdressers not far away so I thought I'd walk there.

Good job I didn't get there, she'd have fainted on the spot. As I was walking down the street to mum's, a couple out walking stopped me and insisted I went with them to their house to get help. Their actions saved me probably. They sat me down and put some towels against my face and called an ambulance. At hospital I had a couple of operations to stitch up my face. While I was there a few friends came up and brought some sniff and alcohol. I had my own room, so I closed the curtains and cracked on. The folly of youth. The police came a few times to question me. I said someone attacked me from behind and I didn't see who it was. They didn't believe me but there was nothing they could do. I had the crime report number which was needed for a compo claim. I put it in and waited. I never saw matey again. I wanted to get away for a while. My mates were in Melbourne in Oz, a good friend of mine Kris was staying at his friend's in Prahran, so I decided to go and visit. Rudeboy was a Techno DJ from Kew in London who had an Oz passport thanks to his mum.

Talking to Kris on the phone he told me that E's in Melbourne sold for $50, about £25. I could get them for £3, so it was a no brainer. I knew what I had to do. I bought 200 E's, Playboys they were called, fucking strong! I stuck them in two tubs of E45 cream and threw it in my luggage. Melbourne, Here I Come. Here We Come!

14

Melbourne, the Pills, Manila and The London Posse, '95

I arrived in Melbourne and walked straight through. No dramas. Rudeboy was DJing that night, so it was back to his house, shower and out with the Garys. The Playboys were strong and everybody was loved up. Get right on one matey! We ate more than we sold the first night, standard. But people were very happy with the quality. After necking pills all night and jetlag, I was fucked for a few days. When I felt better, I got myself out and about to meet Rudeboy's friends. He was a big DJ in Melbourne. The biggest home-grown Techno DJ in the city. And what a city. You have to go to Melbourne, fucking brilliant place. He had the longest running club night on Sundays in the city.

Hardcore Techno. I started knocking them out to his friends. Whenever a famous DJ came to town, he was always on the list to play or warm up the crowd. Dr Motte, a famous DJ from Germany, came over to do his Love Parade party, we helped him organise everything, so we were doing a bit of promoting too. The pills didn't last long, so with the money made I got in touch with my sister's boyfriend and organised with him to send me some more pills. I sent him the money by WU and told him to pack out a couple of VHS tapes with 200 pills. There were loads of people in Melbourne who were up for earning money getting the pills sent to their house. It was easy money, but the thing was we were spending more than we were earning. So we were doing the parcel thing more and more, we'd be sitting, absolutely polo, waiting for the pills to drop, crazy. We were out every night in the pubs and clubs. Our mate Paul had flown over so now there was me, Rudeboy, Kris, Paul and our good friend Pete Lotis, a promoter who lived in Melbourne but was born in England. He had lived in Berlin too, and that's where he met Dr Motte. He grew up in a lighthouse, he was off his trolley but a top man. We became good friends.

Wherever we went people would stop us and ask for the Garys. We were known as The London Posse. One night we were at a club in Prahran, a famous DJ was playing, can't remember who. It was rocking, Rudeboy was smashing the dance floor, getting everyone ready for the main act. It was brilliant over there because we had guest list all the time and they give you drink coupons too, sweet. I was on the dance floor with my fly moves when Boy George walked through the door, saw me, and made a bee line for me. I'd met him a few times in London as we have mutual friends. Big shout out to Nancy Noise! All the people with me couldn't believe it, they were shocked. We had a little chat and off he went. Nice bloke George. I think he was in town to promote a book or something.

We were living the life of Riley. We moved into a lovely big bungalow in the grounds of a Greek Orthodox church, me, Paul, Kris and an Ozzy girl friend of ours. It was massive. We'd have top parties where we'd invite everyone back after a club. Good times. I got a phone call from home telling me my compo money had arrived, so I jumped on a plane and it was back to the smoke. They awarded me £12 grand but because I've got previous for violence the cunts took away 50%, so I had six bags to play with. I bought another batch of Garys, sent some in a parcel and put some in the E45 tub and back to Oz. When I got to the airport, to check in, they went through the transfers with me. To get to Oz back then you usually stopped off three times, one of the stops was in Manila. I thought I'd be there for a few hours, as usual. When we arrived there I went and asked where the gate was for the forwarding flight to Melbourne. The flight was in the morning, I had read the details wrong and I had to stay the night…in Manila…me and the Garys! Fuck. Good work Batman. All over the airport were signs saying 'Death to drug traffickers'. I did not need this. Luckily enough I walked straight through, no problem.

Outside of arrivals in any major city in Asia is a nightmare, but Manila is fucking mental. As soon as I walked out, people were pushing and shoving and trying to get your attention, taxi drivers and tuk tuk drivers selling themselves. One of the taxi drivers who was very persuasive and looked ok said he'd look after me. I needed a friend, I'd got 200 Garys in my bag! He took me to this moody hotel, owned by his second cousin's husband or something, showed me my room and said he'd be back in a few hours to show me the famous Manila nightlife. I wasn't going to argue. I had a shower and grabbed a couple of pills. Get right on one matey. I know, stupid wasn't I? He took me to the moodiest looking club in Manila. It was like a working man's club from up North. Now I like a working man's club, but you know what I mean. There was a stage at the front and a few tables and chairs. He got me a beer and told me to sit down. One by one, loads of girls came walking out, half naked with numbers round their necks. He asked me to pick one. When in Rome and all that. I didn't want to offend anyone, so I picked my favourite. We stayed at the club for a bit and then back to my luxury suite! I gave her a Gary and then barebacked her! Silly behaviour. She could have called the police or had Aids! Being young, eh? I gave her some money for a sherbet in the morning and waved her goodbye.

I waited for my taxi driver/best mate to take me back to the airport and the ongoing flight to Oz. I couldn't wait to get out of there! Fuck knows how much it cost me, my little stop off in Manila, but something to tell the grandkids. As soon as the plane took off, I could relax, only Customs at Melbourne now. I walked straight through, where Kris and Paul were waiting for me, and it was back to Prahran, mate. I was spending a lot of time in E. St Kilda, my lesbian girlfriend lived there, she shared a house there, it was a good place to hide out. We were doing our thing as usual, we'd get a parcel at least once a month. Things were going good until we got a phone call from one of the girls who let us send pills to her house. The Old Bill had intercepted one of the parcels. A policeman had dressed up as a postman and got her to sign off on a parcel of pills. My brother-in-law hadn't packed them properly and they were banging around inside the tapes. Nothing happened to her, luckily enough. She was a prossie and one of her clients was the police captain at E. St Kilda station. When they let her go, she phoned us and told us we'd been rumbled, she didn't give any names. We didn't trust her anyway and the next day we were in Bali. We left everything, the house, girlfriends, the other parcel that hadn't turned up. They probably had that too thanks to my sister's dopey boyfriend! He wasn't the brightest of the bunch. We couldn't risk hanging around. Rudeboy and Pete Lotis took us to the airport and The London Posse was no more!

15

Bangkok, Koh Samui, '95

We travelled around Bali for a bit and then made our way to Bangkok. Most travellers head to the Khao San Rd. Anyone who has been to Bangkok knows about this road. We got three dirty little rooms in a shitty hotel, at the end of the day you are never there, just to sleep and recover. These hotel rooms you wouldn't want to hang around in anyway, if you've seen the film The Beach, you'll understand what I mean. The walls are basically curtains, it's dirty, full of messages scrawled over the walls/curtains, and full of mosquitoes and cockroaches. A shithouse. Anyway, it was cheap.

This was Kris and Paul's first time in Thailand, so everything was new to them, I had been four years earlier with Max so I knew my way about. In the bars and pubs down the Khao San Rd you meet people and plan your trips with them. We wanted to go to Koh Phangan for the Full Moon party, I had been there four years before when I got fucked on the shooms – let's do it again, fuck it! We'd be travelling down south Thailand, then a boat to Koh Samui and then another boat for the party. There was about eight of us travelling together. It's the best thing in the world, travelling around, meeting nice people, obviously a few cocks on the way, but you soon get rid of them, not a care in the world, nice food, cold beer, girls, sunshine and beautiful beaches. What more do you want? Thailand is one of the most beautiful countries I've seen. The people are lovely too. Just don't cross them, they are ruthless. There's a reason why it's the only country in Southeast Asia not to have been colonised.

And they are very patriotic, everywhere you go in Thailand you will see pictures of the King. He's God like and don't dare disrespect him or the Flag. Anyway, back to Bangkok. We had booked the tickets for two days' time so I could show Kris and Paul Pat Pong, the red-light district, it has to be seen. It's where all the entertainment is, it's full of tourists and ex pats working and selling stuff.

The lights are blinding, neon lights flashing, bars and strip clubs everywhere, side by side, street food, girls dancing on stages and boxing rings. There were boxing rings everywhere, Thai kickboxing or Muay Thai is massive in Thailand. In the bigger bars there'd be a ring where tourists can have a toe to toe with a real Thai kickboxer, you'd get the pissed-up Yanks, the English football thugs with their beer bellies and Union Jack shorts, wanting to show what they can do, with bad results! The rules are different, 3 rounds of 3 minutes, only boxing, they can't use elbows or knees and no kicking. You'd get killed by a Thai boxer if you fought him his way, so for the tourists it's only boxing. If you last the 3 rounds you get free drinks all night. So, the first night in Pat Pong I watched as two of my friends got battered by this small Thai boxer, I wasn't having it and helped on by the drink, I jumped in the ring. There's a picture of me somewhere sticking my tongue out to the Thai bloke, while jumping around the ring like Ali. I was in good shape then, I was 24 and in my prime, and I could have a row. Or so I thought. I was winding him up, and in the second round he came close, and I gave him a lovely right hook. He went down. The roars from the crowd boosted my confidence, some say he slipped, No Way! He was done with a proper right hook. Anyway, now he was raging. It wasn't a tourist bout anymore, this was personal. He punched me non-stop in the third round, all body punches and a few to the head, but the body ones were the killer. I was in pain. Thank fuck the bell went. I was hurt but he didn't put me down.

Everyone was cheering as I climbed out of the ring, I turned around to wave to my fans when I saw a little Thai fucker grab my Timberland boating shoes and leg it. Little cunt. Shoeless but victorious, I drank the night away to the sound of Danny Boy. I didn't leave my bed until we left for Samui, I couldn't move. I was covered in bruises; he really was a bad loser that Thai kid. I wasn't looking forward to the journey to Samui, 11 hours by bus and ferry, in a small minibus, with no air conditioning and no suspension, and no toilet! The bumpy roads didn't do me any favours either. When we arrived in Samui I took the boys to the same bungalows where I had stayed with Max four years earlier. Lovely little wooden bungalows on stilts. A nice terrace area with a table and two chairs, where you could sit and watch the world go by, brilliant. You get a fan inside, a mossie net over the big double bed and little table, what more do you want for a fiver? When I was there in '91 it cost £1, but now they had put everything up. Thailand was becoming the new Ibiza. The food and drink were still cheap but everything else was more expensive. The country had seen a massive rise in tourism in the last few years. We hired bikes for our stay, three motocross bikes so we could dart around the island looking for girls, not too difficult in Thailand! Paul was the first to fall in love. He met a Thai girl, who I admit was a page 3 stunner. He fell bang in love with her, straight away. He was always with her or talking about her, when he wasn't shagging her. Obviously, he doesn't know the saying "The pussy is never yours, it's just your turn". After lunch one day me and Kris headed back to our bungalows for a little kip, Paul said he was off to see his future wife. We had already had a few beers at lunchtime, so he was up for a bit of Thai love. "Love you long time". When he got to her apartment in a beachside complex, he knocked on the door and walked in to see a very fat German hanging out of her arse. Shock horror. He turned around and slammed the door shut. Love story over. When me and Kris woke up, he was nowhere to be seen, but we didn't think anything of it and we went to the beach. We were hanging around on the beach all day waiting for him to come back. As it got into the evening, we started to think about what had happened to our old mate Sandy. So we jumped on our bikes and went looking for him. First stop, the love of his life. She wasn't around and neither was Sandy, so we went to a few of our bars and then back to our bungalows. Nothing.

We had dinner, more beers, fucked about for a bit and then went to bed with no sign of Sandy. When we woke up, we saw he hadn't come back, his bike wasn't there, and his bungalow was locked. We thought he might have fucked off somewhere with the bird. We had a bit of brekkers and then got on the bikes again to go looking for our pal. Heading towards the girls place on the other side of the road, we saw some skid marks and some parts of a bike. We stopped to have a look, down the side of the road was a ditch like sewer that ran along the side of the road. We saw his bike in the ditch and heard some moaning, we walked up a bit and about 20 foot from his bike was Sandy. We couldn't stand up for laughing, fucking rolling around laughing. He was fucked. He had spent all night in that dirty ditch, he'd been eaten alive by mossies, but that was nothing to the state of his leg, where he'd come off the bike and slid along the road he'd taken layers of skin off. We tried picking him up, but he said he thought he had broken some ribs. Anyone who has broken a rib knows how painful it is, fucking killer. Even if you fart your eyes pop out of your head with the pain. We left the bike where it was, got Sandy to a doctor, told the police the bike had been nicked and then sat down with a beer to hear Paul's sob story. He told us about finding his bird with a fat German, getting lagging and driving around like Barry Sheene, he had a bit of a wobble on the bike, skidded on the tarmac and ended up in the ditch. Even now, 28 years later he's still got the scars on his leg. Don't fall in love with Thai girls, it always ends in tears and scars!

16

Berlin Love Parade, '96

Dr Motte and Pete Lotis. A recipe for disaster. Throw in Mr C from The Shamen and you know shit's going down. Dr Motte was a DJ and a promoter from Berlin who I had met in Melbourne the year before when we did a Melbourne leg of Love Parade. Love Parade was Dr Motte's baby and one of the biggest musical festivals in Europe. He had started it and now it was a worldwide phenomenon. Pete Lotis was our Aussie friend from England who we had met in '95 in Melbourne. A promoter, the best I've ever met. Very, very smart and a top man. Mr C I had met a few years before through a mate of mine from The Mount, he was Mr C's good mate.

So Pete had turned up on our doorsteps a few months earlier, we were living at Brentford Docks at the time and he stayed with us until he found a job and somewhere to live. While he was staying with us, he told us of his plans to go to Berlin this summer for Love Parade. Hang out with Dr Motte and "Why don't we do a party?". Our own little party during Love Parade. Why the fuck not, we said. Me, Paul, Kris and Pete all put in £500 each and got the ball rolling. We were each given different things to do by Pete and we started promoting the party. Pete went out there one weekend to look for a venue, he used to live there, so we thought he'd be fine. Pete got Mr C on board to DJ the main event, let's say. Colin Dale and Colin Favor were also asked to play, two good DJs from London. The weekend of Love Parade arrived, and we flew to Berlin.

I had got hold of some Garys and asked a mate to stash them in his car when he drove over to Berlin. We planned to eat and sell as many as we could. My mate Scoots was looking after the Garys on the condition he could eat as many as he wanted. When we got to the hotel foyer, we took over the whole hotel. Mr C had arrived with his entourage and right-hand man Layo. It took a while, but we all got a room, I swear I can't even remember who I shared a room with, that's how nasty the weekend was. It was a lovely hotel in the middle of Berlin. Good job Pete, but who the fuck is paying? In the afternoon I drove to the airport to pick up the two Colins.

That night we were Out Out. We were off to see Dr Motte opening the weekend, guest list of course, that's how we roll. Smashed it that night, standard. The next day was Love Parade and sorting out a few things for our moriarty. The Sunday was our day, we got to the venue and started setting everything up. It seemed a very quiet place, but we trusted Pete. It was an all dayer, so the party was starting about 2pm. Slowly a few people turned up, and they were the only ones who came. As the day went on all I could see in the club were our firm and the rest of the mob from London, we couldn't ask for money off them, there were about 10 paying customers. I had a top day and night, I was rocking the dance floor as usual. The pills were going down a treat, selling a few as well, which is nice.

Nobody came to our party, we only found out after that the venue was in East Berlin, the old communist part. No wonder nobody came. Pete fucked up, but as I said I was fucking flying mate, and so was everyone else. Mr C rocked the dance floor.

Obviously, the DJs started to think about their money but that was cut short by throwing another Gary down their scraggers. We'd talk tomorrow, like Fuck. If there's no money, they can't get paid. Anyway, after our do we all went partying to see Dr Motte DJ in a club in Berlin. Me, Mr C and Colin Favor were knocking back the pills like smarties. The other Colin got the hump and fucked off. "We were well loved up" as my old mate Lee Whitlock used to say in The Weekender video. RIP brother. Pete was the face of our party so any problems they had, they could speak to him. We had another top night. In the morning, we were all hanging around the bar in the foyer, some had been up all night, including me, and some were fresh as roses. I spotted Pete having a heated discussion with what looked like the manager of the hotel. He wanted paying for the rooms he had given us, fair enough. Pete calmed him down and said he'd sort it in half an hour. Pete came over to us and told us all to slowly leave the building. In other words, get the fuck out of Dodge!

Me and Mr C and a few others took Pete's advice and slowly walked down towards the car park, underneath the hotel. As soon as we got there we fucking ran as fast as we could. Fuck knows how Pete thought he could pay for all this. That evening me and Mr C got a flight back to London. We laughed all the way back. I left him with his girlfriend, who had come to pick him up from Heathrow. I jumped on a bus, that's the difference of being a pop star! I left him at Heathrow and haven't seen him since, top lad though and a top weekend. Not one of Pete's better parties. Great fun though.

17

Euro 96, Richmond

Looking back, it was a top summer. 1996. The Euros were in England, and it looked like it was coming home. Oasis at Knebworth was tops too, that was a brilliant day out, a crowd of us cracked on through the Saturday night and rolled up at Knebworth about midday for the concert of the decade. Paul's girlfriend at the time knew the head of security so we strolled in right to the front of the stage, I could have spat at Liam if I wanted too, we were that close, but that's another day. I ended up in a prison cell and another trip to Kingston Crown Court.

It was a Saturday afternoon, and the sun was shining in St Mags, we had all arranged to meet up in The Crown pub to watch England v Spain in the quarters of the Euros. It was packed in there, everyone was buzzing. Toilet, bar, football, toilet, bar, football, same old, same old. When England won on penalties the pub went crazy and we headed off to Richmond to celebrate, down by the river. It's only a mile down the road, there was a massive crowd of us, singing and dancing, all the way over the bridge. Richmond is one of the most beautiful towns in London, I'm biased because I've grown up there but on a sunny day, there's no place better. When we got to the Riverside it was just a massive crowd of people, sitting on the grass verges drinking and eating, people outside the bars with beers in hand, and a top atmosphere because England had won. The sun was beating down, I don't know what happens to English people in the sun, but lots of alcohol and sunshine don't mix.

After getting the drinks in, we were outside The White Cross pub minding our own business, when some prick started hassling one of the girls who was with us. My brother got involved, they squared up and my brother gave him a good old Glasgow kiss. Down he went. There were quite a few Old Bill hanging about that day and one of them must have seen something as a couple of them ran over and tried to grab my brother. I turned around and saw my brother being held from behind by a big copper, with his force he was pulling my brother off the ground, I could see his feet dangling in the air. I was about 20 feet away, I ran as fast as I could and punched the Old Bill in the face. He had my brother around the throat, and I could see he was struggling to breathe. He let go of My brother after I punched him. The other copper got involved and he got a slap too. In no time at all a meat wagon pulled up and coppers were everywhere. They tried to get me in the back of the van, but I wasn't having it.

They were hitting me with their batons, I was kicking and punching anyone who came close. Eventually they got me in the back of the van, a couple of them sat on my back and the others kicked the granny out of me. Once the doors were shut, they let out their pent-up anger on me, wankers. The women coppers were getting involved too! Let's just say I got whooped in the back of the van. If you give it, you have to be able to take it, so no complaining from me. After that it was back to the station, charged with five counts of ABH and one of GBH on six different coppers. I was bailed to appear at Kingston Crown Court. I had already been to prison for violence so if I was found guilty, I'd be looking at longer than two years for what I'd done. Against six Old Bill. Not good. I was thinking of having it on my toes but a good mate, Vonny, talked me out of it. It was self-defence, I was helping my brother who was being choked and couldn't breathe.

The first day of the trial, the jury were sworn in. A little man, with a Sainsbury's plastic bag and a Sun newspaper was chosen as the foreman. Touch. A working class man. They usually don't like the police. Good start. When I had been released after being bailed, I went straight to the old Woolworths in Twickers and took some pictures in the photo booth. I wanted to have evidence of the beating I had taken, my face was fucked, and that was down to them. Fact. Those pictures turned out to be very helpful in the case. When it was my turn to give evidence, I told them the truth about what exactly happened. Yes, I did kick and punch Old Bill, but I saw my brother getting lifted off the ground from behind and he couldn't breathe. I gave as good as I got, and I'd do it all again. They hit me, I hit them. Standard. All during the trial the foreman of the jury kept looking over at us and smiling, when he walked past us at lunchtime he'd give us a little wink. Things were looking good.

During the trial something strange happened, my brother was called out of the dock and told his wife had accused a friend of ours of rape. The judge gave my brother time out to go and see his wife. It all turned out to be bullshit in the end. They split up not long after the trial, she had been pissed and took a mate of ours back to hers. Naughty and he should have known better. After the defence finished its case, the jury went out. Me and my brother got Not Guilty on all charges. The police officer in charge of the case came up to me while I was outside the courtroom celebrating and gave me a pound and asked me to put it on the lottery for him. Fuck off. A few days after the case had finished, I was at my sister's house in Fulwell, I was living there at the time. I was just about to walk up the stairs when I heard someone walking down the pathway. As he lent in to put some leaflets through the door, I recognised him, we both stood firm looking at each other through the frosty glassed door. It was the foreman of the jury. Bananas. Fucking crazy. I could hear him laughing as I walked up the stairs.

18

New York, '97

Waiting for the court case me and one of my besties, Paul, thought it would be a good idea to go away for a bit just in case it went tits up. I was arrested in the summer of '96 but the court case was set for early '97. We decided to go and check out New York and stay with a friend of ours, who worked on the futures market in Manhattan. Bradley was smashing it in New York, I met him when he was working for the same company in Sydney. He was part of the group of Essex boys we had met out there, a top lad and a Gooner too. We got on really well and after Oz we had been to a few games at Highbury together. He was always saying to come and see him in N.Y. So, me and Sandy booked a BA flight to Kennedy and flew to the Big Apple for four nights. New York here we come.

Sensibly, we had been up all night drinking and sniffing waiting for the early flight. Not a good move. Travelling under the influence is not recommended! We were hanging. Heathrow was packed with healthy looking holidaymakers. We were fucked. When we got through passport control, we headed straight to the pub and the toilet for a last sniff. Fuck knows how they let us on because we were off our nuts. Kip on the plane, fuck it. Paul's dream was to find an Irish bar in NY with a jukebox and a pool table. Had to be an Irish bar. He wanted to shoot pool, have a Guinness and listen to Jump Around by The House of Pain. And don't forget the chop chop. Brad lived on the Upper East Side of Manhattan with two girls he worked with. Touch. We planned to drop our bags off at his and find the nearest Irish bar. We are simple people. Brad was working, we arrived before lunchtime and headed straight to his. He had left the keys to his place with Mikey the doorman at his apartment block. We were in and out like the SAS. Bags down and out the door. We found an Irish Bar not far away and started drinking, Irish whiskey washed down with Guinness. Banging.

Paul put his song on and started jumping up and down like a cunt. Luckily enough it was early, so it was only us in there. After a few drinks our thoughts turned to the chop chop, someone touched their nose or you see someone go to the toilet a lot and you get the FOMO. I went to have a piss and came back to Sandy having a little chat with the barmaid. He's only asking her where we can get some coca cola. No problem she said, the bloke upstairs sells it. Ten minutes later we were sniffing a $100 bag in the toilet. We were buzzing, all our dreams were coming true. I LOVE NY. The shit thing was though, we had arranged to meet up with Brad for dinner.

He was going to take us to his favourite Italian restaurant on the Upper East Side. We weren't moving from the pub, so he came to get us after work. By the time Brad turned up the bar was packed, Friday afternoon in Manhattan is tops. We didn't want to eat but it would have been rude of us to say no to Brad, first night and all. We had a lovely Italian meal with lashings of vino rosso. When the bill came Brad insisted and stuck it on his company Amex. Sweet. After a limoncello we went to a pub Brad knew and had more drinks. At about midnight we told Brad we were going to meet a friend of ours who lived down on 1st Street. The hood. A friend of ours from Tedds, Rufus, was doing a course at a famous film school in NY. And we said we'd catch up with him when we got there. We should have gone to bed! When we told Brad where we were going, he looked a bit shocked and said he had to get up early the next day for a work breakfast meeting. No probs, he gave us a set of keys and we jumped in a taxi. Rufus was waiting for us in a bar, a very strange bar, it had girls' knickers and bras in the front window and all over the walls inside. Weird. We were playing pool and talking shit, we wanted more gear. It's always nice to try the local cuisine when in another country. Rude not to.

Rufus made the call. I was falling in love with NY, everything's so simple here I thought. The only thing was the stupid fucking moody Western styled doors in the john. Now how can a young man have a private little sniff with doors like that? It's just disrespectful and wrong. Not very friendly. But we had a little pinch anyway. We were smashing it in the toilets and smashing it on the pool table too. The locals loved us and our strange London accents. Fucking bad losers the Yanks, don't like it up them. When we were in L.A., we'd get into fights all the time over pool, here they were better losers. The girl behind the jump was on me too, she kept buying me a drink every now and then. I'm well in here. She was a proper little sort too. The sniff and alcohol were starting to take effect and I was sure I was going home with the lovely barmaid. In my head I could envision us getting married in a lovely little church in Manhattan. That's the coke! If she's buying me drinks, she must like me. Then I noticed her buying other men drinks, I found out that after you buy three rounds, the bar offers you a round.

We got some more parcel in and I became friendly with a lovely Afro-American lad standing on a street corner selling the old wigetty wackety. Jonny was his name and we'd become good friends very quickly. We'd see a lot of each other over the weekend. We got a $50 rock off him and went upstairs to where Rufus was living. It was right above the bar, Rufus knew the owner of the flat, she was a family friend. He was renting a room in the flat which wasn't that big. The girl's boyfriend was always there too, a big fat American fuck. We fucking wound that cunt up, we'd rip him to bits and he couldn't understand. The only problem was that Rufus's room was in the middle of the flat and to get to the toilet the fat fuck had to come through where we were smoking. There wasn't even a door, it was a sheet hanging over the doorway. No privacy! We'd have to hide the pipe double quick when the fat fuck went to the toilet, well funny. He'd be moaning "What the fuck are you guys still doing up?". Fuck off cowboy. I was up and down the stairs a lot, seeing my new Bestie. I went down the last time at about 5am. Jonny wasn't playing ball. He said he was out. Now, it's been two days since I've slept so I should have said ok and gone to bed, but no no no. That's not how it works. I didn't come all this way for someone to tell me the party is over!

None left? He'd have to do better than that. I frogmarched him to his stash house so he could get us some more. It was 5am in the projects and I'm walking right behind him. We eventually arrive and I got the gear. I made my own way back to the flat and cracked on. Literally. We got back to Brad's and tried to get our heads down, but it was impossible with all the class A in our bodies. During the day we'd see the sights, then dinner with Brad, then on to the pub and back to Rufus's flat. Every night. Good times. My mate Paul was in bits the last night, lightweight. He got a nervous tick in NY and he's still got it now, after all those years! A severe lack of sleep, the doc said. It was a hard weekend. "Tell London Mikey says hello." That was our salute from the doorman on Monday morning as we headed off to the airport with our tails between our legs. NY Baby!

19

The Business, '98-2000

In 1998 my eldest son was born. He's 25 now, fucking crazy where time goes. I've got four kids now, two with the ex and two with my lovely wife. My three sons are 25, 19, and 5 and my little girl is 3. I know what you are thinking, I was 47 when my youngest son was born! Fucking bananas. Wouldn't change it for the world though. The three boys were no problem when they were young, but my little girl has been put on earth to test me. A nightmare, although to be fair she's calmed down a lot lately, maybe it was the terrible twos. She's very hard work but we love her to bits, as I love all my kids. She's non-stop, like a whirlwind. Her first couple of years she was always waking up during the night. When I spoke to my mates or family about her they'd say, "She's a girl". What the fuck does that mean?

Anyway, they are all happy and healthy and that's the main thing. The best thing is my two older boys love the kids and vice versa, they came round and had dinner all the time when we were in my town. Me and the ex moved to Italy for good in 1999, I started work as an English teacher, (I still teach in Italy today) and then the following year we bought the business. My ex's family were living in a place in Lazio, on the border of Lazio and Campania. A beautiful place with lovely beaches and the mountains right behind us.

My mum and dad sold everything they had to lend me the money to buy that business and we have been literally robbed. We had our pants taken down over that. My parents sold everything and moved to Italy to retire. When we bought it, we had to pay so much in cash and the rest by bank draft. There were two prices for the sale, one on paper and then the real price. It was all about paying less tax, in Italy it's a national pastime. You can't own the beach because it's government property, you buy the licence and the good will as you are getting all his customers. So, we walked to the meeting with our jackets and bags filled with cash. It was signed off in a Notary office in the middle of my town. We paid £150,000. £75,000 each family. My ex's family gave her the money and told her that was her inheritance, mine lent me the money and they got £10,000 for ten years. My mum and dad made a huge mistake taking her family's advice, we all made a massive error of judgement.

When we bought The Business, my ex was about 28, a young woman with a kid, not married, out of work, so we were told that she'd pay less taxes. So it was put in her name. Big mistake. I wasn't even thinking about it at the time, we had been together for three years and we had a little boy. I wasn't thinking about all the shit I would have to go through in the years ahead. I should have thought more about it at the time but there you go, I was 29 and I owned a beach bar. I was living the dream and didn't think anything could go wrong, but it did. And she kept The Business. After I left her, we had an agreement that she'd give me some money every year and I didn't have to support the kids as she got the money from The Business. It was still 25% mine at the time or so she said! She hasn't given me a penny since 2016, she wanted me back in 2016 but I said no because I was already in a relationship with my now wife. She wasn't happy, I could have stayed and pretended but I couldn't do it. I'd be much better off financially if I'd have stayed but I couldn't do it. There was nothing there.

I think she got the hump that my new girlfriend was 20 years younger than me. I'm older than her mum. My wife's mum is 50 and I'm 52! When we got together, she told me her mum wants to speak to me about my plans for her daughter, I'm fucking older than her! Also having a baby girl upset the ex, she was fine with my new son but as soon as my girl was born, she changed. We don't speak any more, I've never spoken badly about their mum to the boys, never. Even if she is a pain in the arse. All I can say is that if the shoe had been on the other foot, my family wouldn't have treated her like that. How she and her family have treated me and more to the point my mum is disgusting. My dad died in 2007 and thank God my mother got his police pension otherwise she'd have been fucked. As long as my two older boys get their share she can fuck off. I was 29 at the time and an owner of a private beach, I was in my salad days and loving it. I was having the time of my life. I'd ride down to the beach in the morning on my new white Vespa 125, fucking loved that scooter, fucking wankers nicked it from outside The Business, in the week I paid the last instalment on it! You couldn't make it up.

During this time, we had a family holiday in Florida, a week in Florida to see the parks and then a week on a Virgin cruise around the Caribbean.

Obviously with my fucking luck it rained nearly every day on the cruise, we were wrapped in blankets on deck! The first time in 50 years it had rained at Xmas time. In a moment of madness, we bought a timeshare in Florida, in a resort overlooking Disneyland. I spent $15 grand on that, and we didn't go there once. We stayed in Malta for four days in some shitty hotel using the points, fucking Bananas. I took my eldest son to India for two weeks with friends of mine and their kids. Top holiday that was. We hired a minivan for two weeks with an Indian driver and we travelled around Rajastan, stopping off at different places for a night or two. Brilliant memories from that holiday, my son had his first shave in India. Such a peaceful place, even the poorest people have a smile on their face, for them this is just a passage on to the next life. Us in the West have a lot to learn from them.

20

Dam 2001. My Stag Do.

So, I was getting married to the ex in September 2001, the stag do was in Amsterdam for three nights. Me, Sandy and my Italian brother-in-law left from FCN in Rome to meet the motley crew in Dam. My brother, my cousin Paul, my brother-in-law, and all my friends were meeting up in the cheese and ham for three nights of debauchery, that only Dam can offer! We got settled in our rooms which means bags down and out the door. I wasn't going to share with my Italian brother-in-law, No Way. He was a civil lawyer in my town, and I don't think he would have been pleased to see what we got up to in my room, so I got him a single, on the floor below me. FOX! I was sharing a room with my old sparring partner and partner in crime, Vonny.

We all met up in Dam Square and got straight on the Heineken. Anyone who has been to Dam knows that a pint of Heineken in Dam Square is probably the best beer you'll taste in your life. No pun intended. People kept turning up from London, the pub was packed, and we were all looking for the chop chop. Which isn't difficult to find in the cheese and ham. Von had a contact who lived there and soon enough we all had a bit of packet in our pockets. After a few hours my ex-brother-in-law was getting restless, in Italy they don't just drink to get pissed, they eat too. Weird I know, but there you go. So, he said he was going to find something to eat, he asked where I'd be in a few hours and I replied, "Right here". Anyway, we cracked on, there were so many of us that the group started breaking up into little cliques, three or four people at a time, off doing their own thing. We had arranged to all meet up in the evening at a certain bar. The state we were in, we weren't eating and also now someone had got hold of a big bag of MDMA. The old Mudma. The old Mandy. But I had to make an effort for my ex-brother-in-law, so we went to an Argentinian steak house to keep him happy. My mate Roy could eat even high on coke, so him and my ex-brother-in-law scoffed down their steaks while I messed about with mine. After dinner it was down the pub to meet the mates. There were loads of different groups in the pub, hen nights, stag do's and a lot of the locals. My mate Paul was there, jumping around as always and he saw Kris slip off to the toilet downstairs. Paul was all over him, smashed the door down and joined Kris in the toilet.

Greedy fucker. Kris racked up 2 fat lines, Paul done both of them, that's one of his jokes! Paul thought it was coke but it was MDMA and that shit burns your nose. He let out a scream and came running up the toilet stairs into the bar and punched one of the locals in the face. For no reason. The place went mental. There are some heavy people in Dam, so you have to be careful. We got kicked out by the bouncers, fair enough. We had to drag Paul out, by now he was fucked. We got to another bar and Paul was gurning like a MOFO. Basically, he was off his fucking head! He was all over the gaff. There was a bunch of girls on a Hen do, all dressed in pink with different nicknames and shit. Paul wouldn't leave them alone, he was being a nuisance, standing in the middle of them, rubbing himself. Well loved up. Then he started to touch their tits. Not very appropriate. They started pushing him away and screaming at him, the bouncers got involved and we were out again, two pubs in one day and we'd only arrived this morning!

That was night over for Paul, me and Kris dragged him back to the hotel and locked him in. He was a danger to the public and to himself. He collapsed on the bed. Paul's first night in the cheese and ham was over. The next day we regrouped and started all over again. Same shit, different day. But now we had tales to tell from the night before. What happens in Dam stays in Dam. There was talk of Trans and Midgets, all a bit weird. My ex-brother-in-law went off to see some type of museum or something and we cracked on, literally. Me and Von had found some bones and headed back to our rooms. Dem bones Dem bones, Reggie Guts used to say. RIP. Smoking that pipe can make you a bit para. Some people are ok, like myself, and some people like Von get a bit didgy. I used to call him Didgy Rascal because whenever he got on the bones, he went AWOL. He couldn't go anywhere this time because we were locked in our room, but in London if you turned your head he was gone.

Then it came, the dreaded knock on the door. We quickly took the wet sock off the smoke alarm and stood still. Bang Bang. It was my ex-brother-in-law, shit. We stayed as quiet as possible until he went away, he must have known we were there, but he fucked off. When the bones were finished, we relaxed a bit, which was difficult. After a bit, we had a shower and got ready for a big night. We had heard Roger Sanchez was in town, only one of the best DJs in the world. We all met up in Dam Square, hit a few bars and then headed off to where Sanchez was playing. When we got there, there was a queue all round the block.

Back then my mate Von was the spit of Goldie, the Drum and Bass star from England, same gold teeth and everything. Nobody was getting in to the club, they were picking and choosing who to let in. It was a one-off Sanchez set in the Dam and everyone wanted to see it. There were about six of us lot waiting in the queue, but nothing was moving. My ex-brother-in-law and my brother were getting impatient. You could see the bloke with the guest list letting a few people in. Me and Vonny looked at each other and headed for the guest list. We had already spoken about him pretending to be Goldie so let's give it a fucking try. "Hello mate, hello mate, I'm Goldie, the DJ, Goldie, Goldie". I was pushing him in saying "Come on, he's on the list, I'm his manager, I phoned earlier", with the confusion and people getting frustrated outside, they just let us in. We were in. I felt a bit guilty about leaving everyone outside, but it didn't last long! Fuck 'em. It was kicking in da club, loads of people with their hands in the air, rocking the dance floor. The club was tiny, the dance floor even smaller. We went right up to the front, where Sanchez was and stood in front of him. London's in the house, we screamed as we were dropping our fly moves. We were fist punching Sanchez as he dropped the tunes. I went to get us a couple of drinks, Von got bit by a bar when he was young and hasn't been back since!

On the way back I saw a little parcel of something on the floor, I bent down and picked it up. It was a small plastic bag with pills in it, Sweet. I had a good look, showed Von and they were defo E's. Nice. We necked a couple and sold the rest. Top night. The next day we relaxed, drank, and ate something and then got back on the chop chop. Standard. It was the last night, so we were taking it easy, we said goodbye to everyone and headed back to the hotel for a kip. We were flying back to Rome in the afternoon, so we had the morning free. We decided, or my ex-brother-in-law did, to go and see Anne Frank's house on the way to the airport. I was still hanging from the night before but wanted to keep my ex-brother-in-law happy. I've been to the Dam three times and I've seen fuck all, only Anne Frank's house. Fucking depressing! Yes, I've read the book and seen the film, but the place is just depressing. The rooms are all tiny and it was very claustrophobic, no air in there and I was sweating, getting all that Ecstasy out of my body. I wanted out of there. On the way back to the airport I heard my ex-brother-in-law speaking to his wife "Yeah, great time but it's funny, the English just don't eat" Ha Ha.

21

Barcelona, '04

My old mate Kris di Mure from Ham was getting married in Brighton in a month or so and had decided on a stag do in Barca. Euros 2004 had started and also there was a famous Music festival on in town at the weekend. Sounds good. I bought a couple of tickets for the festival because a rapper from London I like was performing. Roots Manuva. Three nights in Barca. Come On. The only trouble was I was sharing a room with my old friends Yinks and Scoots. Double trouble! Kris had deliberately stuck the three troublemakers together. In a shitty hotel on Las Ramblas. Before I got the plane from Naples, I had put 5 grammes of primo coke up my arse. Fuck all that hunting for the gear in Barca, I'll cut out the middleman. I wanted to be prepared. 5 g's wrapped in two jonnies then in a kinder egg and then in another jonny and up my arse. As soon as I arrived and got through customs to the other side, I was straight in the khazi. Out you come. Straight in a cab and off to meet my friends. I got to the room, and they were waiting for me. We had a couple of fat lines each and then went to the pub where the rest of them were getting ready to watch England's first game.

Brilliant timing. London in da House. Football, toilet, drink, football, toilet, drink. Same old, same old. The bar had the footy on a big screen outside, it was a lovely afternoon., sun shining, near the sea, what more do you want? It was rammo outside, loads of people. As we were celebrating an England goal, everyone was jumping up and down, some nasty little Spanish gypsy grabbed a handbag from under a chair and legged it. I was on him, I was the record holder for three years in the Richmond Borough races at 75m when I was a kid, they used to hold it at Twickenham Rugby ground. I was the only one who ran bare foot. I chased him, and right behind me was the girl whose bag it was. He wasn't getting away, he let go of the bag and I gave him a kick up the arse for his troubles. All sorted. The girl was obviously very happy (I think she wanted Dicky Love), she thanked me all the way back to the bar and bought me drinks the whole time we were there.

The next day, Saturday lunchtime, Kris had organised a get together to celebrate his upcoming wedding. A stag lunch, let's call it. Me, Scoots and Yinks didn't make it. I'll explain why. The night before me and Scoots were out and about looking for trouble, walking the streets at fuck knows what time in the morning. A half caste kid walks past me and I recognise him. Jonny from Amsterdam. This kid was the boy who had supplied us with all our drugs in the Dam three years ago. I shit you not. I was blown away, what a fucking piece of luck. He said he remembered me, but I couldn't give a fuck if he did or not. I remembered him. Jonny. It's what the fucking time it is in the am and you appear.

There is a God. I got straight to the point. Where are the bones? And why are all Cilla Black dealers called Jonny? My man in NY was called Jonny too. An easy name to remember maybe. Jonny saw a pound note when he saw one and my credit card was waiting to get smashed. Scoots didn't have a penny, but tonight was on me. When he had it, everyone had it, top man Scoots. We followed Jonny to his mate's house. The Doc lived not far away, and we were promised bones and girls. What more does a man want at FKWT? Obviously, he was called Doc for a reason. His chemistry skills at washing up coke. We smoked non-stop for a couple of hours, now it was morning time. Yinks got in touch, and we invited him round. My credit card was getting smashed. There was a bank opposite Doc's house and every hour or so Scoots went down to get another €200.

Lunchtime was coming and it was getting nearer and nearer to the lunch date with our friends and the groom to be. We were hanging and in no fit state to mix with normal people. Bloody disrespectful really and not very nice. I know, but that's what drugs do to you, you don't give a fuck about anyone else. They turn you into a very selfish person. So we didn't make it to his official stag do lunch. I honestly feel shit about that even today, and it was nearly 20 years ago. But me, Scoots and Yinks were in no condition to sit and eat or converse with ANYONE. We weren't even talking to each other while we were smoking. Just moody facial expressions and thumbs up. Fucking sad. We crawled out of Doc's after lunchtime and made our way to where they were carrying on the party. Las Ramblas, what a shithouse. If you go to Barca, stay away from Las Ramblas. Full of dodgy people from Napoli selling drugs and pushing you to brass houses. We ended up in a moody disco on the Ramblas and then on to a brothel, to finish the night off. Scoots insisted. Waiting in the reception we got talking to a group of scousers, one young kid came out and high fived the man talking to me. "Well done, son" and he introduced us "Meet my future son-in-law" Legend. Genius. Fucking bananas!

22

Castelvolturno, '04-'08

What can I tell you about Castel Volturno? It's a town in Caserta, Campania in South Central Italy. A town on the Mar Tirreno Sea near Napoli. It's famous for a massacre that took place by the Camorra Mafia against African immigrants in 2008. This town was full of Africans long before they started coming over in boats. Some work and try to lead a normal life, but it's mostly drug dealers and prostitutes. Back in the day it was a well-known place where you could go 24h a day to get whatever you wanted. Things changed after the Camorra sent a gang of men armed with machine guns to teach the Africans a lesson.

They were allowed to sell drugs there only on the say so of the Casalesi, an organised crime group from Casal di Principe in Caserta. There was an argument about prices, or they were sourcing their drugs elsewhere. If you've seen Gomorra, the Sky series, they touch on this in the first season. The day after the massacre, where 7 innocent Africans were killed, the community there rebelled and started causing trouble in the town. Burning Italian flags and shit. The Italian Army was called in and order was restored. The government called it 'Strade Sicure' which means 'Safe Streets'. I was gutted because I went up there the day after knowing nothing about the killings and I was met with Italian tanks in the middle of the road. How was a man to get some bones? A mate of mine I played 'Calcio a Cinque' with told me about the place, and I started going there when things got dry in my town. It took about 45 minutes from my town but in my Touareg I'd get there in 30. Usually lagging off my head, overtaking cars at speed. Crazy shit.

Stupid shit. One of the very first times I went there, I met Cooch. He was a tall skinny black man from Senegal. He used to love me because every time I saw him, I'd sing the Arsenal song, "He comes from Senegal, he plays for Arsenal, Vieria…" he used to love that. He had a dodgy leg, so he limped a bit, but he was very well respected. I've seen him pull a knife on a few people, he didn't take any shit from anyone, and he ran the little place where he lived. He lived in an old, deserted hotel once owned by the Coppolla family. It was derelict and he lived and worked by the swimming pool. He was an expert at washing up coke and making bones. He knew I was a good earner, so he'd look after me when I was there, and we'd sit up all night smoking. After a while he'd get some girls over to keep us company. Nice clean girls. I've seen some crazy shit there, people would turn up at all hours to buy drugs. I've seen someone overdose on heroin and he was on the floor dying. A few of the Africans picked him up, called an ambulance and left him on the pavement outside on the main road. God knows what happened to him!

Another time I went back to my car in the morning and all four of my tyres had been slashed. I was gutted, you just don't need it, do you? I went back and told Cooch, he took me to a friend of his and got me four new tyres. I used to go there with a boot full of wine and beer, blankets and old clothes to hand out to the people there. They had nothing and were basically living rough in old buildings. I remember once I took my brother, my sister, and her husband to Castel Volturno. A family affair. Me and My brother left my sister and her husband in the car, and we went to get some chop chop. I think we left them for a couple of hours in the car, just off the main road. Out of order really. They were not happy when we got back. Until we got the packet out. I used to take all my mates from London who came over, they couldn't believe the place. One time I took a couple of my friends from The Business, young kids, probably about 20 at the time. I introduced them to Cooch, it has to be said that they were good boys and didn't indulge.

On the way back with the parcel, we were stopped by the 'Carabinieri', the military police in Italy. There are seven or eight different police forces in Italy, these are the most dangerous. We had to get out of the car, I had already stashed the gear up my arse but it's still a worry. Out of the car and documents out. In Italy you always have to carry a form of I.D. on you. One of the officers looked at my mate's I.D. and asked him if he knew a doctor in town with the same surname. Yes, he said, it's my dad. Touch. The officer knew his dad very well, back in the car and off we go. Well happy. Another time I was sitting smoking with Cooch when the curtain he had up as a door was pulled aside, a big white Italian walked in and said "Police, documents". I fucking froze, then he and Cooch started laughing. It was one of the Camorra hoods checking up on things, you'd see them walking around now and then.

The Africans could only sell drugs bought from

the Casalesi, they had a free run but under the control of them. That's why the massacre took place, the blacks started getting too big for their boots. Seven innocent people were killed in 2008. All of the murder squad were arrested and are serving life in prison.

23

Cassino, 2010

We shouldn't have gone. In hindsight. 'La Vecchia' who owned the bar where we used to drink, told us not to go. I call it a bar, it was a tiny drinking hole where nobody went and that's why we drank there, we'd meet up after work and drink very cheap Peroni beer. It had one fruit machine and an ice cream fridge. There were about five or six of us who drank in there regularly. It was a tiny place, it was on a main road, it was difficult to park so you hardly got any normal people in there, only us. The old woman made enough money out of us lot to stay open. Anyway, I think it was a Thursday and me, Gianni and Gianky were knocking back the birras and discussing if we should go to Cassino.

It's a famous city in Italy, one of the bloodiest battles in the 2nd World War took place there. Some friends of ours lived there, six brothers. A lovely family who were clients of mine at The Business. One of them was celebrating a birthday and we wanted to go and join them. We were already over the limit, but we weren't pissed. La Vecchia told us not to go. It took half an hour to get there, it's one long road from my town. So, we jumped in the Touareg and off we went. We stopped off a couple of times for a birra, when you're on a roll it's difficult to stop but it was fucking silly, drink driving. We got to Cassino, found the bar they were in and cracked on. Champers, cocktails and whisky. Not a good mix. Now, I can drink as much as the next man but with whisky I turn into an animal. My Scottish blood!

A couple of the brothers went to school with Angelo Ogbonna, the West Ham player who comes from Cassino. He was in the bar celebrating the birthday with his sister. Anyway, I don't remember much about the evening, I know I had an argument with a bloke about something and we went toe to toe over something trivial. As usual. We moved on to another bar, and another. So by now I'm fucked and I want some chop chop. Asking about but no luck. It started pissing down outside, the weather in Cassino is like English weather, always grey and cold and wet. We decided to leave before the weather got worse. Gianni started driving towards my town, because I was fucked, five minutes into the journey I told both of them my intentions of going to Castel Volturno to find some sniff. They didn't want to go so I pulled the car over and pulled them both out of the car, violently. I gave Gianni a kick up his arse too. I told you I became a prick on whisky. I left them in the middle of nowhere in the pissing rain. Disgusting behaviour.

I jumped back in the car and drove off towards the golden goose. I was all over the place, zig zagging in the road, fucked. I was on the wrong side of the road flashing people to get out of the way. The police were coming towards me, and I kept flashing for them to get out of my way. I remember a couple of police cars pulling me over and after that it's all a bit of a haze. They told me to stop the engine, show some documents, I said no, why? Then they told me to get out of the car, again I said no because it was pissing down still. That's when they dragged me out of the car, and it all went off. They called for backup because three or four of them weren't getting me in a van, no way. It took about eight of them to get me in the back of the van. I totally lost it when they got me back to the station. I smashed up the holding room where they were keeping me waiting, they eventually strapped me to a table with three belts and called a doctor who put me to sleep with a jab. I don't know if that's legal but that's what they did.

The morning after, they took me straight to Cassino prison. I was in there two nights when on the third day they took me to court. I walked in and sitting in front of me as the judge was my brother in law's brother! I knew the judge very well and he was a lovely man, I still see him about every now and then. Obviously, he couldn't hear the case because he knows me, so they got another judge in. My brother-in-law was my lawyer. It was all a bit surreal. I pleaded guilty to all charges and got a suspended sentence. My wife's family weren't too happy, and neither was she. It is what it is. Until it isn't. I realised that I was exaggerating with the drink and the drugs, so I went back to London to start NA meetings. I got off the drinks and drugs for eight months. Very boring, and it's difficult to socialise when you aren't drinking. Although the NA meetings were very good, and I met some nice people.

24

Open Heart Surgery, 2021

At the beginning of 2021, in the middle of Covid, we were back living in Italy. We had been living in London on and off from 2017, our beautiful baby boy was born in Rome in 2018. A miracle baby as my wife had complications near the end, she had measles and pneumonia seven months into the pregnancy. They rushed her to hospital in Rome, where they made her sign a piece of paper signing away the responsibility if one or both died, as they fought to save them both. He was born two months premature and was in an incubator for a month, my wife was in a coma for 10 days. I stayed in a hotel for a month and was back and forth visiting them both in different parts of the hospital, at different times. My wife got out before my son, he was about two weeks old when my wife saw him for the first time. Anyway, mum and son made a full recovery and are doing very well thank you very much. A lot has happened since Cassino, we can talk about that another time!

In January 2021 I was very sick, I was waking up soaking wet from sweating. I'd have to change my T-shirt two or three times during the night, and I had a constant headache. I'd wake up with a 40 temperature and uncontrollable shakes. I went to the local hospital three or four times and each time they said it was Covid. One time the shakes were so bad we called an ambulance. I was lying on the bed shaking like someone fucking possessed, like the girl in Exorcist. They took me in, checked me for Covid, I was negative and sent me home again. All the symptoms were like Covid, the high temperature, the sweating, the headaches so everyone just thought it was Covid. January and February passed, and I was constantly sick. A good doctor friend of mine who works in the local hospital was worried about me and said something wasn't right. He said he was going to get me into hospital for a few days to do some tests. He brought me on to his wing and put me in a room on my own – luckily, I knew the head of his department, I used to teach him English. They did tests on my lungs, on my brain, on my stomach and everything was clear, fuck knows how that went with the brain! Then we went to see the cardiologist. As soon as she attached me to the machine, she saw something.

Endocarditis. Never heard of it. And I'm an English teacher. It's when bacteria forms a crust around one of the valves on your heart. It stops the valve from closing properly and all the bad blood comes back into your heart and bloodstream. Or something like that. She saw it straight away. If you catch it early enough it can be treated with pills. Mine was far too advanced and she said that I'd need surgery. I was shocked. Heart surgery? Fuck that. It didn't hit me until I went back to the room, and I was on my own. The tears started. I was fucking scared. Felt fucking lonely at that moment, but you come into this life on your own and you go out on your own. I got myself together and called my wife. It was bollox because she couldn't visit me because of Covid. She used to come and stand outside my balcony, and we'd talk on the phone whilst looking at each other.

Bless her. My friend at the hospital with the cardiologist started looking around for the best hospitals. A name that kept coming up was Dr Massimo Chello, who worked at Campus Bio Medico in Rome. He was the best. The head of Cardiology at the local hospital knew him personally and said he'd speak to him. So we had to wait. I stayed another three days in hospital, bored out of my nut. They were brilliant in the hospital, keeping an eye on me, but I thought I could be at home instead of taking up a bed. My friend wanted me to stay in hospital until I went to Rome, but we didn't know how long this was going to be. So I discharged myself. They gave me medicine to take and told me to be careful and to come back if there were any problems. I went home and I wasn't a very good patient. I was anxious to get the op done asap. Someone I knew from my town, who was my age, had died recently from the same illness because they didn't catch it in time. He was 50. It was a stressful time. For everyone.

Every day I was waiting for a phone call, weeks passed by, it was doing my nut in. I'd be on the phone to my doctor mate every day, I probably stressed the fuck out of him too. He'd say just be patient, they'll call you, don't worry. Don't worry? I was sitting there flapping. After three weeks I got a phone call on a Friday evening telling me to present myself in Rome, at Campus Bio Medico to have a Covid test on Saturday morning. My eldest son offered to take me to the hospital, so he picked me up, took me to Rome, I had the test and, on the way back we stopped off at Trigoria, the training facility for La Magica, Roma. We took a few photos and headed back to my town.

The hospital phoned the same day and told me I was negative and to get myself back up to Rome on Monday morning to be admitted. Bring a bag, she said. Campus Bio Medico is like a Swiss hospital, it was incredible, so clean, so big and so efficient. It's a non-profit University Hospital that is run on donations. Everyone from the porters at the entrance to the surgeons were so professional. An unbelievable place, especially in Italy. The nurses were lovely too, most of them fresh out of uni and very keen to learn. I was very surprised by the whole set up. On Monday evening I was told my operation was on Wednesday. On Tuesday evening I was shaved all over by a female nurse with my 85-year-old roommate looking on. She even shaved my balls, everywhere. She explained that it's dangerous if a hair gets in the wound during the operation. I was feeling ok running up to the op.

The afternoon when they called me down is when I started thinking about things that could go wrong, or not seeing my kids again, my girlfriend and my mum and family. My sister, who has been a massive part of my life. My younger brother, who has always been my best mate, even if we argue now and then. My sister's husband, is the best brother-in-law you could ever have, I've known him since I was 12. A top man. My Scottish cousin Paul who is more like a brother to me. Will I see them again? I was waiting outside the operating theatre on my own and I realised I had my Lyle & Scott boxers on, I was supposed to be naked. I took them off and threw them in the bin. Three or four nurses came into the holding room and pushed me in to the pre-op theatre. "Okay I'm going to sedate you now, think of lovely things" were the last words I heard, and I was gone into that lovely soothing deep sleep. Opiates, ya cannae whack em!

I woke up with five or six doctors and nurses standing over me. I had tubes and monitors all over me. On the back of my head was a battery that controlled all the tubes. It was taped to the back of my head, and it was fucking uncomfortable. I couldn't move. Those hours in the post-op were the worst. I didn't know what time or what day it was. But I was alive. The day past and in the evening they took me to the rehab ward. There were about 10 of us in there. Funnily enough, the man on my left was from Gaeta, a town that borders my town, and the man on my right was from my town. Small world. I did two days in bed, no moving. Torture. I was attached to so many tubes that even if I wanted to, I couldn't get up. The first time they said I could sit up and eat on a chair next to the bed, I was well happy.

Sitting on my own, on a chair, was heaven. The little things in life, eh? I felt free. The next thing was going to the toilet on my own. After a long time of not going to the toilet, the time was near. By now I had my property back and my phone. Now I could speak to the kids and my girlfriend and phone muvva. The old boy from my town, in the bed next to me done my nut in. He kept asking for "Una bella Coca Cola fresca". A lovely cold Coca Cola. He had just had an op, so there was no way he was getting that, but he asked the nurses every hour or so. A bit senile, the old boy. Prof Chello came round every afternoon with his doctors to check up on us all. He went from bed to bed, keeping us updated on our situation. The turnaround was incredible, if you were deemed fit enough you were moved to a regular ward. I had the operation on the 24th of March 2021 and I was discharged on the 1st of April. Yeah, I know, funny day! The Prof said that because I was younger than the other patients I could rehabilitate at home. The older people had to go to a rehab facility for two weeks before being sent home. The worst thing was taking the two tubes out of my stomach, they sat on me and pulled them out with great force and quickly stitched me up. Very strange feeling. The doctors said after a year I'd be back to normal and would be able to lead a normal life. It's been over two years now and I still get tired walking up stairs and my running days are over. But I feel fine. My wife picked me up which was emotional, we went for a panino and a birra. Felt good. Life is good!

25

My Arrest – Rebibbia – Extradition

It was the 3rd of November 2021, and we were in my town, we had just dropped off my youngest son at nursery and it was dark and grey and pissing down. Unbelievable rain. We went to the supermarket to get some food; we were going to have pasta tuna for lunch. In Conad, the supermarket, we got a call from my wife's mum. She said the Carabinieri had been round looking for me. As I've said before they are the military police, they take care of the most important cases. We didn't live with her mum, but my residency is down as her address. So, when we finished the shopping, we drove to the station. I went in there and asked for the officer that came looking for me. I knew something was wrong when I walked into his office and the tallest policemen I've ever seen came and stood by the entrance of the door, which meant I was closed in. The captain then started going on about how he knows that I'm a nice person, but he has an International Arrest Warrant from Interpol for Drug Smuggling at an international level. So, I'm under arrest.

It was weird because they didn't actually arrest me, not like in England where they read you your rights, there was none of that here. I was fucking shocked obviously, I've never been involved in drug smuggling, only a few pills when I was younger! I was under arrest for a ton of coke seized in Madrid in 2019. I said what? They showed me the paperwork and I saw a name I knew. Now it all made sense, I understood why my name got involved. While I was working for a company owned by a mate of mine, I had put money in his account. I put £110,000 in his account from my business account from January 2019 until April 2019. He got nicked with six others in Madrid in May. So, the 'SEROCU' South East Regional Organized Crime Unit put two and two together and got five. They said I was the money man for the group and financing the drugs. I don't know how 110 bags can get you a ton of gear but there you go. So, the Met police were extraditing me back to London. Extradition only usually happens for Murder or Drug Smuggling. Bananas.

My girlfriend and my baby girl were still outside waiting for me, oblivious to the fact that our lives were going to change. The Old Bill in my town were good as gold and let me phone her to explain that I'm basically fucked! I called her and told her I'd been arrested; she couldn't understand. She was in shock. I told her I needed a lawyer and a bag made up of some clothes and toothbrush and shit, because I was going away for a bit. She was crying and drove straight to her mum's to leave the baby. I had to sign the warrant to be able to get a lawyer. If I didn't sign, I couldn't get one. I wasn't signing anything until I saw a lawyer. My wife's mum sorted out a lawyer and he phoned the station to speak to me. He told me to sign the paper because without my signature he couldn't start working for me. He wanted four grand as a starter. My girlfriend came back with a bag for me, she came in and we had a little chat, I told her to get rid of certain things and not to speak to anyone.

When she left, they took me upstairs to take

pictures and prints. There were two officers chatting to me and making jokes, calling me 'El Chapo'. Pricks. They never handcuffed me while I was in the station and I still had my phone, so I called my two sons and told them what had happened. That was a difficult one. They were phoning around the prisons looking for spaces. Cassino prison was the nearest but there was no room at the inn. Then came the call, Rebibbia in Rome. I had heard of this prison through a tv series 'Romanzo Criminale'. I was put in the back of a Carabinieri police car and driven to Rome by two of our best! I still wasn't handcuffed. I wasn't going anywhere anyway. They had machine guns in the car! That was one of the worst drives I've ever had. It was still pissing down outside, a horrible day.

We got to the prison, and we went through all the procedures, security, doctor, etc. I was to do two weeks isolation because of Covid. So I was stuck in a big cell, usually for three people, with a tv, two beds, a toilet and a sink. The water was drinkable, which was a life saver. No hot water and no shower. It was a shithouse. The food was crap, worse than England's prisons. By contrast the food in the hospital in Rome, where I had my operation nine months earlier was better than most Italian restaurants in London. Anyway, I was in jail, not a hotel. I was in isolation, I couldn't speak to anyone or get out of the cell. No phones in an Italian jail, just a payphone. I couldn't get in touch with my wife or my mum, they didn't know what was going on. In England there are phones in your cell, you pay for credit, they vet the numbers and you're off. Not here. The phones help a lot, especially for the more vulnerable people, it saves families. My little boy was suffering badly that I'd gone missing. He was crying all the time, I can still see his little face when he waved goodbye to me at nursery. Now fuck knows when I'm going to see him again. In the month I was in Rebibbia I didn't speak to anyone on the outside.

Being in a foreign jail is very strange. After two weeks of doing fuck all in a cell on my own, I was moved on to the wings. My lawyers were working to get me house arrest until the extradition. I was put in a four man cell with two old Roman gangsters and a younger bloke who was basically their joey. They treated him ok, but he was just a gofer, go for this, go for that. The two old boys were in their 70s and were doing 30 years. Fuck knows what for, I didn't ask. I could write a book about the things I saw in Rebibbia. Fucking mental experience. I done two nights with the old boys, they looked after me because I had nothing, they treated me like a house guest. My money hadn't arrived yet, so I had nothing, they fed me and made me feel at home. I had one of the best 'Amatriciana' I've ever had in Rebibbia. It's a Roman dish with pasta, tomato sauce with guanciale, which is pig's cheek and pecorino cheese. It was banging. One of the old boys made it.

Better than a restaurant. In the cells in Rebibbia you cook for yourself, if you have the means. They turn the toilet into a kitchen, with gas camping cookers, and more pots and pans than I've got at home. You can buy anything you want in jail in Rome. You can even get food delivered from outside, anything you want. Like Just Eat, etc. Bananas. They wouldn't let me do anything in the cell as I was their guest. The bed I had taken in their cell was a boy's who had been in there with them for six months, that morning he just got up and moved cell. Without saying a dicky bird. He had moved into a bigger cell right opposite from the one I was in. The first and second day he kept coming in the cell, nearly crying, asking for forgiveness from the two old boys. They weren't having any of it, I was there now, and they said I was a good person and respectful and that was it. This prick wanted to come back into his cell. I thought I was going to have a problem with him, I fucking didn't need this. The old boys didn't want to let him back in on principle. I spoke to the OGs and said I didn't have a problem swapping with him because I didn't know anyone there, so it was fine with me. I told the bloke that I was only moving because he had been in there before me, otherwise I wouldn't have moved for anyone. The old boys appreciated my stance.

So after two nights and some of the best food I'd ever eaten, I was off. I had already met the three boys who were in the cell opposite and they were sound. They were three boys younger than me from a place called Aprilia near Rome. It was a cell for six people and there were four of us now. It was brilliant, they were good as gold. All of us had a job to do in the cell, a proper little democracy. One cooked, one cleaned the cell, one set the table, one did the dishes, it was organised chaos. I still didn't have any money in, but they treated me as one of them. They shared everything they had, no questions. It was like eating at home. Pasta to start, meat for seconds and then a piece of cake or something that was sent in by one of their wives or family. We'd get up in the morning, have an espresso and a biscuit, clean the cell, have a shower and then go for a walk around the football pitch for an hour or so. You'd usually walk with a couple of people, that's when you get to know them, when you're walking around talking shit. I didn't last long because after a few weeks I got my house arrest. I was in Rebibbia about three weeks, and I'll never forget how those people treated me. That week on the wing showed me how even people in prison and suffering, still look out for the next man. I saw a lot of trouble between the north Africans fighting between themselves, but I didn't see any grief between Italians. It was like their beefs were left outside and everyone just gets their heads down to do the bird. 'Head Down, Chin Up' as my old mate Jimmy says.

So one morning I was in my cell when a screw shouted down from the top of the wing, behind the gate. 'Inglese Libero'. Everyone was buzzing for me. It's mad how people, even when they are stuck in there, are truly happy when someone gets out. My friend Ale took my bag and walked me up to the gate. Everyone came out and shook my hand as I passed their cells. One of the old Roman boys passed me smiling and gave me a slap on the back. I was taken to a holding cell and waited for fucking ages for the police to pick me up and take me back to my town. They eventually came and after the signing of all the paperwork and property shit, we were off. When we got to my town the Penitentiary Police had to hand me over to the local police, the Caribinieri. So now there were two cars driving around my town looking for my wife's mum's house. The policeman from my town said he knew the road but kept getting lost, I was in the back, and he wasn't listening to me. We finally arrived outside, two police cars down this small street. The locals loved it. I was being bailed to the mum's house because that's where my address showed up at the council offices. We had our own flat, but it would have taken too long to sort out and it would have delayed me getting out. So fuck it, I'll stay at my wife's mum's. They knocked on the door and nobody was in. For Fucks Sake.

We had to go to my house to get my wife. We went up to the house in two cars, much to the delight of our neighbours! A Carabinieri car and a Police Penitentiary car waiting below the apartment for my wife to come down. Obviously, she took a beard, and I was sitting in the car fucking embarrassed! Not a good look but it is what it is. I wasn't happy. I wanted to go back to my place not her mum's. My wife came down, had a word with the Old Bill and told them to follow her. Now we were three cars. Fucking hell, anyone else want to join in? My mum and her partner had flown over from Spain to give my wife a hand with the kids, so she was at the house with them. My youngest boy had been suffering a lot since my sudden departure. We are always together, he's my little wing man. He took it hard, and little did we know what was coming. We got to her mum's and the tag people came round, tagged me up, walked me round the house and pissed off. We were alone. Well except for my wife's mum, her partner, my mum with Jeff, the two kids and my wife's sister turned up too. We could have a little party. My two older boys came round to see me as well. Full house! Obviously, I wasn't allowed to leave the house. It was lovely to be back with the wife and kids but there was always that thought of when they were coming to get me. I was at the house 10 days when my brief phoned me and told me they were coming the next day. Lovely. I had only got an English brief when I got out on home release. If certain people had livened me up and told me what was happening in London, I could have had a brief in place and my defence sorted.

The Pen Police and the Carabinieri came knocking at about 7.30 the next morning to take me to Rome FCN airport to meet up with the Extradition police from the Met. They frogmarched me through the packed airport, handcuffed, fucking embarrassing, up some stairs and into an office. I waited ten minutes, they said goodbye, someone took my tag off and I was handed over to England's finest! There were three of them and they were brilliant with me. Waiting to board the plane they gave me some food and drink, and talked about their night in Rome, paid for by the taxpayer. Fucking top job, extradition police. Travelling the world to pick someone up and bring them home, with enough time for a night out and to taste the local cuisine. Lovely jubbly. We were first on the plane, and we were occupying four rows of seats at the back of the plane. There had to be three empty rows between me and the public. Fucking mental. I'd have flown back on my own, if they'd have asked! Waste of money.

When we were buckled in the top man told me that they didn't care what I did and they didn't even want to know, their job was to hand me over to the Met, nothing else. They told me about their pizza in

Rome, all expenses paid of course, and how beautiful a city Rome is. They had had a good night out on the government. Good luck to them. I'm thinking of my wife and kids and wondering what the fuck is going to happen to me. We got back to Heathrow police station, and they handed me over, each one of them shook my hand. I was familiar with Heathrow police station because my dad was there for years. We used to play table tennis at the station. That won't be happening today. It was late when they booked me in, and it was the first time I was charged with 'Importing drugs at an international level'. I replied, 'Not guilty to that anyway'. It was a Thursday night and I'd be staying here until court in the morning. Guildford Crown Court for a bail hearing.

I had two moody microwave curries and got my head down. The curry wasn't too bad actually, wherever you go in the penal system they have a variety of ready-made meals to offer. English breakfast, which is banging, different curries, lasagna, spag bol and a veggie one. I'd remember to try all of them while I was in! So, it was straight to Guildford in the morning, refused bail and sent to HMP High Down in Sutton. I was refused bail because they said that false passports and guns were found in the flat in Madrid and that with my money and connections, I was a flight risk. Money? I was fucking polo, all my money went to the Italian lawyers! I still owe them fucking money! At Guildford waiting to be shipped to High Down I was in a holding cell with a young traveller kid, it was going to be his first time inside. We started chatting and he turned out to be a good kid. We were banged up in the same cell for two months, so you get to know someone. In those first two months in High Down, he didn't have one shower! I could write a book about what went on in High Down, but that's for another day.

In short, I was in there from the beginning of December until about April the 11th, when I got bail. I had three different cell mates, a gypsy, a Jamaican crack head, and an Indian bloke. You can't call me a racist! I smashed the telly up one night in with the gypsy because he used to watch tv all night and sleep all day. One night I told him two times to turn it down, the third time I picked it up and threw it on the floor. I was gutted though because it was early Saturday morning and MOTD was on that night and Football Focus at midday! The Jamaican tried to large it and jokingly rushed me, I was up and ready in a second and he backed down. That was the end of him. The Indian guy was the best. The gypsy and the Jamaican slept all day and watched tv at night. I think they were both a bit scared to mix with people outside. The Jamaican on his Playstation all night, like a big kid. He was in his 40s! The Indian was clean, respectful and made me feel very welcome in his peter. I was in the cell one day when a screw came round and told me I was supposed to be at Guildford Crown Court for my trial. Nobody told me. I had to pack up all my things because I knew I'd be going to Wandsworth after court, as anybody on remand after April 1st, went to Wanno. I said goodbye to everyone, I met some good people in High Down, and I hope they are all doing very well.

I went to court for a pre-case hearing and then

off to Wanno. When I got there, we were all in a holding cell and we knew we would be banged up with someone in here. Fuck me, there was about 30 of us in there and only one looked normal. There was one other lad who looked ok, but he was a traveller, they usually stuck together. And he had Turkey teeth, you couldn't look at him without laughing. You couldn't be banged up with him, with those fucking teeth, nobody is getting to sleep. We spotted each other across a crowded holding cell, and it was instant. He shouted across 'Don't I know you mate?' That old chestnut. I thought sweet. We got chatting and he was sound, I'd never seen him before in my life but I'm a good judge of character just by speaking to someone for a bit. But now we were together. Wandsworth is a shit hole. Dirty tiny fucking Victorian cells. Fucking cold as well. I did two days of Wanno to Guildford for the case. Up at 6 and then just waiting around for the bus to leave. We were always late, we were getting to Guildford about 11am every day and the judge was fuming. Judge Black. During the lunchtime break one of the guards came in with a cup of tea and told me my brief wants to see me and he's got some good news, the guard was a lovely lady who I had got to know coming back and forth to the court. She said that it's nice to see good things happen to the nice people. I thought what the fuck does that mean. Half an hour later I was taken to see my Junior QC, Will. 'You've got bail' he said. I said, 'How did you do that?' Five months in High Down and we were asking all the time for bail but nothing. Will said 'I asked'. The judge had had enough of the lateness and my defence said that the case wouldn't be heard if it carried on. They would guarantee I'd be there at 8:45 every morning so we could start on time. My so-called co-defendants were both on bail, so why not me.

This is why I'm still pissed off with certain people, because if I had known about the charges and that the SEROCU were looking for me, I could have had everything sorted beforehand. The head of the unit had stuck her head on the line by extraditing me, and with all the costs and whatever she wasn't going to agree to bail me. I was getting out. This was the start of a two-month court case that had its ups and downs, for all my family.

26

The Trial, 2022

The afternoon I got bail I walked out into the foyer of Guildford Crown Court, where the free people were. What a feeling. My brother hugged me, and my mates Max, Jim, and Dave were all there to whisk me off to the pub. We headed to the Red Lion in Tedds. In the car I phoned my lovely wife to tell her I was out. She thought I was out for good, and it was all over, I fucking wish. I explained to her that I got bail and was staying at my brother's. Luckily enough when the judge gave me bail my brother was in court and he said I could stay at his. Without asking his wife! Now I was out on bail my wife and the kids could come over. But first things first, let's have a Guinness. Or ten! A few other friends came down to the pub to say hello, any excuse to get out the house. It was a Thursday when I got bail, I had to go on Friday and then there was a week free from court because two of the jurors had Covid. Sweet. I had to sign on at Staines police station every Saturday and Sunday between 12 and 2pm. Pain in the arse, but there you go. There was a pub near the station, and we'd get there for 12, have a few Guinnesses and then sign on and fuck off. That first day out I was buzzing, there was a little firm of us now in the pub.

My brother pissed on that fire when he said the tag people wanted us at home by 8 o'clock. To tag me up. The bail conditions were 8 at night until 6 in the morning, I had to be at home at these times. On the way back to his we stopped off for another pint and he ordered in a packet. He made the call! I was on a camp bed in the front room, but it was better than High Down, any day. In the morning my mate Dave picked me up and we went to Wetherspoons in Guildford for a lovely breakfast with a Guinness to wash it down, all for under a tenner, lovely. After court on Friday, we went straight down the pub in Sunbury. Drinking and sniffing all weekend. My brother took me to the station on Saturday and Sunday, no dramas. On the Sunday we started drinking and sniffing early with the leftovers from the night before. Keith Richards said always have a tickle in the morning of what you were on the night before, to get you back in sync. And he's a fucking pro. Early starts are no good because you have to crack on. So we did, all day, and then back to his for 8. When we got back to his it all kicked off. Me and him started arguing, then his wife got involved, so I told her where to go. 'Don't talk to my wife like that' my brother said. 'Don't talk to my husband like that' she said. Fuck off. They hated each other, my brother had been sleeping in his son's bed for the last 10 years and now they were playing happy families! Fuck off.

We started fighting, he punched me in the face, I kicked him in the head and threw a pint glass at him. My brother-in-law had to come round and split us up. The kids were there and got involved, unfortunately his daughter jumped in the way when I tried to kick him in the head. Shit happens. My brother-in-law dragged me out of the house, and I stayed at his. I woke up Monday morning feeling like shit, I had a black eye where my brother had landed a good shot. By now I had gone three or four days without my meds, and I was feeling shit, all my meds were at Wanno with my possessions, so my sister drove me up there to get my stuff. I was in a right state. Fucking took ages to get my stuff, and when I got it, I was fuming.

All of my letters, my photos and the book I had written, were all gone. Some cunt was running around in my Polo trackies but I didn't give a fuck about them, but the private stuff, sentimental stuff, fucking pissed me off. There's fuck all you can do about it so fuck it. On the way back to my sister's house I asked her to drop me off at Kingston hospital because I wasn't feeling too good. Luckily, I didn't have to go to court this week, turning up with a black eye is not a good look. On the Wednesday I had to go to central London to meet my QC for the first time. Mr Andrew Campbell-Tyke. What a top man. We went through the case, and he said I had to trust him and that I had to be totally honest with him. My wife and the kids were coming the next day, so I was buzzing. I went to pick them up from Gatwick. I was outside the Arrivals waiting for them when my youngest son came walking through, spotted me and came running into my arms. We had been speaking every day, even when I was in prison, he thought I was working in London, bless him. He had probably suffered more than anyone. I picked him up and held him, it was beautiful. We stood and hugged, all of us, for about five minutes.

Six months had passed since I walked into the police station in my town, seemed like a fucking lifetime ago. I was now staying at my sister's house because of the fall out with my brother. That would have been my first choice anyway because they've got a bigger house, so it all worked out. I didn't really get on with my brother's wife anyway, always trying to keep up with the Jones's. My brother-in-law had a granny flat on the side of his house, so we were in there, sweet. It was lovely to be with the wife and kids finally, the wife had been through so much grief just to get the passports for her and the kids. In Italy the father has to sign off on anything for the kids, I mean it sounds right but what if you don't speak to the ex anymore and you don't know where he is? They needed my signature on the paperwork because you have to have the father's permission to leave the country. All this was down to fucking Brexit, before they could have flown to England on their I.D. cards.

I can't even remember how we sorted it, but we got it done. We had a few days together, took the kids to Legoland on the Saturday and then it was back to court on Monday. I had to get to Guildford every day from Sunbury where my sister lives. So either my sister or my good mate David would pick me up and drop me off at Walton train station for the 8:06 to Woking. I'd get to Woking at 8:18, walk to the platform and get the 8:26 to Guildford and arrive at 8:33. I still remember the times now! The train station is behind the court, if the trains were on time, it was a very simple journey, a relaxing journey, it was just what was happening in court that fucked with your head. I was sitting in the box with two people I had never met before, my so-called co-d's. My co-defendants. Mark and Donna. Donna was the wife of the bloke nicked in Madrid, whose bank account I had put money in. No ill feelings towards her, she had fuck all to do with it. They arrested her just on the off chance she knew what her husband was doing. Fucking out of order, she had three kids at home. And just by looking at her you could tell she wasn't right, mentally. The whole thing had taken its toll, they had been arrested in May 2019 in Madrid and here we were in April 2022 in Guildford. Bananas. The other one, Mark, knew most of the boys involved but was small fry in the big picture. I got to know him quite well, he was a bit older than me, a Chelsea fan, overweight like most Chavs, but he was good fun. His son and his father-in-law were with him every day, he just seemed like someone who had got in way over his head.

We used to go to Wetherspoons every lunchtime, a couple of Guinnesses and a 6-inch pizza, bang fucking bang. Well, we didn't know how all this was going to last, so we tried to enjoy each day as much as we could. Even if you are looking at 20 years inside! Now, I had nothing to do with International Drug Trafficking, I didn't know any of them personally but as the court case went on there were a few strange coincidences. Friends of friends and shit like that, and a few of them lived on the patch too. In the prosecution's case there were two OCGs, Organised Crime Groups. The Madrid group and the London one. All I was doing was using this bloke's bank account to pass through a bit of money, I didn't know he was running around Madrid with Colombian cartel members playing Tony Montana. I had 10,000 pages of evidence. Involved in the court case were the American DEA, The Colombian National Police, The Spanish Guardia and SEROCU from England. Not a bad little firm that. I did not need this, Rodney!

During the trial the lady, Donna, was having a few mental health problems, I don't know if she was trying her luck or whatever, but she asked to be stepped down on health issues and the judge agreed. She was bailed and would have another trial. And then there were two. So it was me and Mark left. The trial lasted two months. The security at the court said it was the longest they could remember. When it was my time to be examined, the prosecution QC let his junior question me. Looking back, he threw his junior in there because he knew they had no case. The junior QC was older than his superior, he was a fat, bumbling man. Walpole of the Bailey, I called him. I swear he tried to act like him, I don't know about Walpole, he was more like a Womble the way he wobbled around the court. Although the original was much more well prepared. I don't want to say I had the better of him, but I defo held my own. I was telling the truth about what I was doing, so nobody could trip me up. Walpole was onto a loser and his boss threw him to the lions. During one of our stand-offs, he said he thought I was a very intelligent man, I said no, you're the intelligent one otherwise I wouldn't be where I am, I'd be in your place. Shut him up. He kept talking about the money laundering, at one point the judge stopped him and asked him if I was on trial for money laundering or drug offences because he hadn't asked me one question about the drugs. Please get to the drugs, the judge said. Well, they couldn't because I had fuck all to do with it!

All the members of the English OCG had

already pleaded Guilty to their offences because they were banged to rights. They had all had Encrochat phones taken off them when they were nicked. I saw all the evidence, they were taking pictures of the gear in Colombia and writing messages on WhatsApp. I went through all the evidence a few times and when my name turned up or was mentioned by Flynn, it was obvious what I was doing with him. The Madrid OCG had their phone tapped at the house they were staying in, so Flynn was talking to his wife about what we were doing, which had fuck all to do with drugs. He'd call me King because we'd usually meet in Kingston for the drop. The head of the case for SEROCU, Lisa something, had a hard on for me and I never found out why. They had spent a lot of money getting me back, so they weren't letting me go. My QC Mr Campbell-Tyke argued that anyone who had half a brain could see I had nothing to do with it. He was nearly held in contempt of court for calling the prosecution case against me a witch hunt, likening it to American politics and Fake News. He had to apologise to the prosecution, he done it in his own special way. To see Mr Campbell-Tyke at work was fascinating, I got to know him, and he was a lovely man and very professional as was his junior Will.

Lots of different things happened in the trial, I fell out with a very good friend, people let me down but that's for another day. I just wanted this trial over so I could get on with my life. My co-d Mark was worried, his defence was 'yeah I'm a cheeky chappy, I know a few bad apples, I've sold coke in the past, but I had nothing to do with the big one'. It was a gamble. The prosecution and the defence finished their cases, it was down to the jury. You never know which way it's going to go. My QC hated waiting outside so he'd go home. I didn't want anyone at the case, so I was on my own. The longer the jury are out, the worse it is because it means they are not sure. If they can't get a majority straight away, then something's wrong. The jury asked to be let in to ask a question and went out again. Every time you get called in you think the jury has decided and your heart starts pumping a bit faster, which is not good for me! They couldn't agree on a majority, so it went to 10-2. The jury were out over a week, one of the longest waits they've had at Guildford.

On the 24th of May 2022 we were called in to the court, it was nearly 4 o'clock so I thought the judge was going to send us home again. No, they had made a decision on their verdict and my life. 'Could you stand up and face the judge please.' 'Do you find the defendant Guilty or Not Guilty of the offences?'…..'Not Guilty'. Thank fuck for that. Yes. Yes. Yes. Mark was sitting down, he jumped up and gave me a high five. 'Mr Hobbs can you stand up' blah blah blah, I was in a daze, all I heard was Guilty. Mark fell back on to his chair, I turned to him, slapped him on the back and told him he'd be fine in prison. This was his first time. 'You can leave the dock', as I walked out, I turned to look at the jury to say thanks, but nothing came out. Mark's father-in-law fist punched me as I walked out. I felt gutted for him. I didn't even say thanks and goodbye to Will, my junior QC, that could wait. I wanted to get as far away as possible. I phoned my wife and told her it was over; she was with my sister and they were both screaming and jumping about. I went back to my sister's and we had a take away, I didn't even want to celebrate. Mark was going to jail and the people who had put me in this position had disappeared and not come through with their financial promises. I had lost my job in Italy due to the extradition, and my reputation had taken a battering thanks to the negative newspaper articles in my hometown in Italy. Anyway, I had my wife and kids and my family, I thought things would get better, little did I know. But at least I was free.

27

Back to Italy, June 2022

After the Not Guilty we stayed another week at my sister's and at the beginning of June got a flight to Napoli. We were going home, together. We flew into Napoli on a Friday evening, when I got to passport control, I knew there was a problem. They took me into the little police station in the airport and started asking questions. They said that on their computer I still had an electronic tag from Rebibbia. I explained to them what had happened. How could I have gone to England with an electronic tag from Rebibbia? I told them I was extradited from Rome and had spent five months in jail in London and was found Not Guilty after a two-month court case. One of the policemen was thick as shit, and wouldn't have it, he thought I was on the run from London! His boss came down and explained to his dumb officer that if they had given me my documents and passport back, I was free to travel. He insisted, he wanted to speak to someone in London. At midnight, on a Friday!

That's not going to happen! My wife and two young kids were tired, my wife was getting angry. The big boss said I could go, the thicko was still going on about speaking to someone from London. His colleagues were laughing behind his back and telling me to go. So, I hadn't been back five minutes and already there were problems. I didn't need this shit. My Italian mates Ennio and Angelo were outside to pick me up. It was gone midnight, but it was brilliant to see my old mates again. We have been friends for

20 years and they'd do anything for me. We were all knackered. We got back to the house after 2am, it was nice to be in a familiar bed, and to be on our own for once. The next day I went down to see my friends at 'The Chiosco' for an aperitivo, I'd arranged to see my son too. Then we went to my favourite restaurant in my town, 'Zi Anna', to have my favourite dish, 'Prawns and Courgettes Pasta'. Banging. I could see that I was getting a few strange looks, as if to say, 'How come he's back?'. It was summertime and there was no teaching work, my ex-wife hasn't given me any money for seven years from the Business, that WE bought together. We had to get through the summer until the schools started. We went to Spain to visit my mum and her partner. My sister and her husband and their youngest kid came over too. That got messy, it was a houseful and there was a lot of drinking. Good fun though. As the summer finished, I was waiting for a job from a state school but after my arrest that didn't arrive. So I got in touch with my old school friends in Sessa.

So, in the middle of October in 2022, it was back to work. After a year with Open Heart Surgery, six months in prison and losing my job, what did the future hold for me and my family?

The End?

I'm a bit older now and I've got two young kids. I've slowed down a lot, I still like a Guinness and a laugh. I wish I'd never have taken that first line from Scoots at the Gatecrasher Ball in '88, at the Hammersmith Palais. But there you go. I've got a few regrets but I'm not going to bore you with them. I've spent too much money on that shit gear, wasted too much time trying to get it, standing outside pubs or darting round people's houses. And it all ends with a dirty fucking hangover in the morning. Those fucking headaches used to kill me. And blood on your pillow from your nose bleeding. Glamorous eh? Just say fucking NO! That's what I'd tell the young uns. It's prison or the death bed. Just this year I've lost three good friends, one was a really close mate, Lee Whitlock, we grew up in Twickenham together and shared a special bond. The Arsenal. I'll never forget those times with The Arsenal Away Boyz singing and dancing. RIP brother. Friends are dropping like flies, The Acid House scene has got a lot to answer for!

Go to school, get an education, learn a trade, work, buy some property and keep your fucking nose clean. But don't forget to have a fucking good time doing it. Big love to my beautiful wife, who has stood by me through everything. My lovely four kids. Three boys and no problems. One girl and it changes everything. Bloody hard work women. To my mum who continues to show us all love after all the shit we have put her through. To Jeff, my mum's partner, you are the best. To all my friends and family, Big Love. To the ones who have let me down. Karma. And it's your loss. And finally, to Dave 'Lurch' Beasant. Do you remember me?

Chioggia, November 2023.

Synopsis

"Head Down, Chin Up" that's what my good pal Jimmy from Putney wrote to me when I first went to jail. He's twenty-five years clean now. Top man. The screws used to think I was famous in The Mount prison, the amount of mail I'd get. It was a sound bit of advice though that I still use now.

That was thirty years ago – where have all the fucking years gone? I've never been famous, but I've lobbed Dave 'Lurch' Beasant, who else can say that? I've been extradited from Italy on an International Drug Trafficking charge, I've owned a two hundred metre private beach. I've had open heart surgery, I've put my family through loads of shit over the years and I ask myself, was it all worth it? Yes, it fucking was! 'Get right on one matey' we used to shout at the raves, well now, 'Get right on this book!'. I'm just a normal bloke, trying to tell my story.